"Nothing has a stronger influence on children than the unlived life of a parent."

Carl Jung

Dominique,
Thank you for being You!

Bobby
10/12/10

the 101% you

Bobby Bakshi

Resonant
Insights
PUBLISHING

Resonant Insights Publishing
16904 Juanita Drive, Suite #197
Kenmore, WA 98028

www.resonantinsights.com

Cover and internal graphics designed by Denise Alvarez

Designed, printed, and bound by Vladimir Verano
at Third Place Press, Lake Forest Park,
on the Espresso Book Machine v.2.2.
thirdplacepress.blogspot.com

In memory of my father:

Thank you for your many gifts.

Contents

You deserve your success
and so does everyone else.

Acknowledgements

I am deeply grateful to many people who inspire me to be my best and from whom I continuously learn. Here are those that come to mind right now as I write this:

All my efforts start with my wife Judy Bakshi. She is my continuous supporter and she's got my back. From the first time I met Judy in 1987, she has been relentless about one thing: she believes in me. If it wasn't for her support and encouragement I would not be writing this book or creating the giving enterprise that Resonant Insights LLC is becoming. She came aboard 100% with my choice to leave Microsoft after an eight-year career there, despite our having three little kids to support. Judy is my extra 1%, my Power of Inspiration. Judy has also spent countless hours in reading and editing the many iterations of this book.

My mother Pushpa, my sister Rajni, and my brother Rajiv have all been a complete blessing in my life and on this journey of reinventing me. If Judy has suffered the pains of my going from v1 to v2 and v3 and so on, my family lived with my 100% self as v1 from birth. For that I am grateful and blessed. They too have my back and believe in me.

Bill Dare is a dear friend and elder who inspires me with his humility, integrity and commitment to mentoring me to be me. He's my external "Jiminy Cricket" (a.k.a. Pinnocchio) who holds me high by believing in me and at the same time challenges me to look at things from different perspectives. He is integral to my circle of support with which I am so blessed.

I owe my deep gratitude to scores of friends from the many communities I belong to. It is hard to name them all as it would take up many pages and I want to honor them here. To all of you who have been there in my darkest moments and helped to shed light on the beauty within me, I bow to you and acknowledge you for the amazing person you are.

To close, I share this ancient Tibetan blessing for all who read this book:

May you be filled with loving kindness.

May you be well.

May you be peaceful and at ease.

May you be happy.

INTRODUCTION:

The 101% You invites you to tap into a powerfully generative experience in your life and use it as a constant reminder to have the best life imaginable. Use the Seven Steps and the accompanying invitations to ask yourself deep questions that can be applied for greater success in all areas of your life. The intention is that by the time you have completed the exercises; you will have clarity of purpose and already see shifts in how you **ACT** in the world:

Awaken to your best self.

Commit to your desired outcome.

Thrive in what you create.

Your 101% is not about perfection. It is about doing your best at any given moment.

#1. You can only give a maximum of 100% of yourself toward anything.

#2. Be clear about what matters most and be 100% focused on just that.

#3. The 1% in **101% You** is the Power of Inspiration, the spark that delights.

The extra 1% works through us. It is that unexpected inspiration we didn't think we had in us. It shows up in unexpected ways that we could not have imagined in advance. It gets sparked by something we feel, a connection with someone or some event that leads to brilliance. We also inspire others, as others inspire us to go beyond what we could imagine on our own. The Power of Inspiration is what turns the impossible into the possible.

My Peak Event

The Seven Steps of **The 101% You** emerged from a very powerful peak event I accomplished. During a week-long personal leadership workshop at a rustic ranch in California, I had the opportunity to do a series of ropes courses. Each one of the four events were challenging for most people, as they certainly were for me. However, I knew from the start of the day that one event in particular would be my most challenging. I quickly found out that I was drawn to that event as a symbol of the gift, the prize, I sought. The event was to climb a fifty-foot telephone pole, balance on the top of the pole and then leap to catch a trapeze bar, if I chose. Here's how it went for me:

Step 1: My Intention.
> *I got clear about what I wanted of the event.*

Step 2: My Choice.
> *It was my choice to do the event.*

Step 3: My Commitment.
> *I committed to another person exactly what I wanted.*

Step 4: My Work.
> *I climbed the pole.*

Step 5: My Power.
> *I hoisted myself onto the top of the pole.*

Step 6: My Integration.
> *I balanced myself on a shaking pole.*

Step 7: My Gift.
> *I turned to face the trapeze bar and leaped to catch it.*

The intention of **The 101% You** is for you to leverage this metaphor and practice the tips by doing the individual exercises suggested.

Peak Events

I call my pole experience my Peak Event. We have all had them. As you read this book and do the exercises, start to think of one or several Peak Events that you know at your core were pivotal for YOU. This experience should have all of the following elements:

- You felt it was *impossible to achieve* when you set out

- You were clear what you wanted was *your desire and your choice*

- You draw *great positive energy* and delight whenever you recall what you created

For some it's a physical achievement (e.g. running a marathon), for others it is an intellectual win (e.g. a good grade on a challenging course in school), or it can be a creative endeavor (e.g. a painting that just flowed from you). It's a moment when you 100% knew you did your very best. Only you needed to know that it changed you to the core of your being.

Keep Your Peak Events in mind as you go through the Seven Steps and the accompanying invitations. Share it with us at *www.resonantinsights.com/resources/your-peak-event* when you are ready. You will have an opportunity to review your Peak Events throughout the book and in great detail in Chapter 7.

How to use this book?

The 101% You is designed to be a workbook. Each chapter starts with a portion of the story from my Peak Event, climbing a 50-foot pole and leaping to catch a trapeze bar. Your investment in having bought this book is far more about the time you put into the invitations I propose you do than the cost of the book. Here is our suggested approach to getting the most of your investment:

1. After reading the Introduction, **read a lesson a day**. Each chapter is broken into a few sub-lessons to illustrate how that step works. Take it one sub-step at a time.

2. **Answer the invitations** (questions and exercises) with each lesson you do. Do them right away while the lesson is fresh. Use the space provided and start a journal to compliment your work.

3. **Document any 'aha' moments** and personal revelations that come up as you read each lesson.

4. **Find a partner to share your responses** to the exercises with and support you in accountability to make progress with the lessons.

Why Invitations?

I call the questions and exercises 'invitations' because we are ALWAYS at choice. Hopefully the questions and exercises will evoke feelings and thoughts that assist you in looking inside yourself more deeply than you might have before. You also get to choose what and with whom you share what you learn about yourself. We invite you to have a trusted partner to share your experience of this work with.

Be ⇨ Do ⇨ Have

The common pattern many of us practice consciously or subconsciously is: *"If I DO abc... activity, I will HAVE xyz... thing, and then I will BE happy/free/creative."* Instead, imagine if you started with a state of BEING happy/free/creative, leading you to DO what brings you happiness/freedom/creativity and resulting in HAVING the life you desire. Having is great—it's only human to desire the material things of this world. Own it and celebrate the desire. It gives you focus to strive for an end outcome.

A state of being is a choice, a mindful approach to how you "show up." *It is your choice.* The same situation can be approached in a multitude of ways. How do you choose to approach a situation?

Angry or calm	Aggressive or confident	Competitive or focused
Confused or articulate	Hateful or peaceful	Selfish or generous
Shaming or complimentary	Criticize or constructive	Deprecating or generating

At Resonant Insights, we empower people to be their 101% best. We are always at choice in every situation in life, even those where we feel we don't have control. We choose how we "show up" for the many situations that are presented to us in our day-to-day life, and sometimes those truly challenging situations. A state of being can be positive, negative or neutral. You get to choose.

> *"Men often become what they believe themselves to be.*
> *If I believe I cannot do something, it makes me incapable of doing it.*
> *But when I believe I can then I acquire the ability to do it*
> *even if I didn't have it in the beginning."*
> ~ Mahatma Gandhi

This quote is packed with lessons. Here's one interpretation:

1. *At birth*, we all start by **being** 100% perfect just as we are.

2. Knowing this perfection, we can choose to **do** the things we believe we are to do.

3. The result is **having** the life we desire.

Be Your 101%

The focus of Resonant Insights is on your achieving Your 101%. It takes every one of us being our best to have the world we all desire. We are inundated with messages that sell us on being someone or something else. We are lured into separation—fat/skinny, strong/weak, rich/poor, stylish/unstylish, etc. These messages constantly train us to compare, condemn and criticize others. Actually, that finger-pointing is more about us than the external world we are pointing at.

Each one of us has a unique place on this planet. No one else occupies that space. There is only one You. Beyond your name and personality which is unique, every cell in you is 100% unique. There is so much focus put on being yourself, being authentic. Why is it so difficult?

Looking at the 100% more deeply:

- No one else can ever be exactly You.
- You possess innate gifts that only you can bring to the world.
- Everything about your gifts is 100% you and cannot be replicated.
- There is no need to compare yourself against anyone else.
- You can only be who you are.
- You are full of strengths and opportunities.
- Your gifts are Your Work. Live it 100%.

We are programmed to take on so much from others—the things we "should" **Do**, the things we "should" **Have**—and then, maybe, we have a right to **Be** ourselves. That programming gets ingrained at a very early age and becomes your pattern. You will have an opportunity to examine your patterns/programs in this book.

Just as a brand can reposition itself, so can each individual person. Just as customers can discern when a brand is being oneself, people can tell when you are being authentic. In the end the truth is YOU know when you are being authentic and when you are not it causes disease. You are your only judge. You know when you are being 100% of who you are meant to be. That is your primary job.

Remember: There is only one you, ever. You are perfect just as you are. You are 100% the best you there is.

The Power of Inspiration: The Extra 1%

The 1% in **The 101% You** is the Power of Inspiration. It's that unexpected delight you never saw coming. Some call it synchronicity, some call it a miracle, and some call it luck. It works through us and through those that support us. Your focus on what you want attracts the resources that you need. You don't need to know "how" when you set a vision, an intention, for what you want as an end outcome.

You rarely have any direct part in making it happen – other than being open to it and welcoming it. These are the times when the Universe is demonstrating that it is always conspiring for your highest and best good. Never sell yourself short. Add "this or something better" to any positive desire you have. Leave space to welcome an increasingly thriving life, beyond your imagination. As humans, we can only wrap our minds around something familiar, that we already believe in. See and believe that which seems impossible, can be possible.

The movie "*Invictus*" is a great example of the Power of Inspiration and how it shows up:

> *Nelson Mandela recognized South Africans bonded over the sport of rugby. François Pienaar, Captain of the South African rugby team, was inspired by Mandela's modeling of forgiveness and compassion in tackling the changes he desired for his nation.*

> *Pienaar and his team made the "impossible" possible and won the 1995 Rugby World Cup. They gave it their 100% best by doing the things they needed to be a world-class rugby team. They practiced and stayed focused on their end intention to be champions.*

> *Mandela evoked the added 1% that Pienaar likely never imagined he had in him. Mandela demonstrated self-leadership and led by example, in his state of being. The doing actions, for Mandela and Pienaar, fell into place naturally, once there was a clear intention: to win the World Cup (for Pienaar); to model unity (for Mandela).*

Remember: It only takes one person/event to turn the impossible to possible, for others to believe and follow.

The following examples turned the impossible into the possible:

o   Run 100 meters in less than 10 seconds?   Yes we can.

o   Travel by air?   Yes we can.

o   Humans land on the moon?   Yes we can.

o   A phone for everyone?   Getting there quickly.

o   Climb Mt. Everest?   Yes we can.

Leveraging The 101% You

Lev-er-age: (v) verb (used with object): to exert power or influence on

Most of us get the concept of leverage when it comes to financial and company assets. Do you apply it to your own life, your desires, and being the 101% you? When we operate 100% from our strengths, we are leveraging our power to whatever we put our mind and heart to. Add that spark of the Power of Inspiration, that extra 1%, and The 101% You is leveraging all of who you are. Leverage is a key ingredient to turning the impossible into the possible. To illustrate:

> *The Egyptians used human labor (around 2600 BCE – 2500 BCE) to construct the pyramids and other amazing engineering wonders. With the help of leverage. By using ropes and planks to hoist stones of impossible proportions, they made it possible to construct amazing wonders, one stone at a time.*

Today, the leverage of human potential shows up in many ways. It starts one person at a time. Movements are based on the leverage of like-minded people, complimentary skills and timing. Leverage is a key ingredient to accomplishing the impossible. Microsoft does it with its vast partner network, Coke does it with its global distribution, Facebook does it with millions of dedicated fans, Richard Branson does it with the vibrant and unique energy of his brand; and these are just some examples.

As you read **The 101% You,** and do the exercises, continually tap into your strengths that you can leverage to take you forward. This applies in all areas of your life you choose to upgrade.

You are not your past.

You are not your future.

You are who you THINK you are.

CHAPTER 1

STEP 1:
YOUR INTENTION

BE CLEAR ABOUT YOUR DESIRED END OUTCOME

As I waited all day for my chance to climb the 50-foot telephone pole, I knew this event was going to be big for me. Something inside me was convinced this was a pivotal moment in my life. I was full of fear. The fear of failing (not falling) was over-whelming my thoughts.

Before I stepped forward to climb the pole, I knew exactly what I wanted. I wanted 100%! I knew that far too many times I had come so close to getting exactly what I wanted and then would sabotage myself. I've had many 99% moments and I was always left feeling incomplete. As I stood in anticipation of my event, I knew exactly what 100% was for me—to make it through all stages of the event, culminating in grabbing the trapeze bar with both hands. THAT was what I wanted, what I really, really, really wanted! No compromises. Nothing less! If I didn't get what I wanted I knew I would be lying to MYSELF if I convinced myself with lines like "I gave it my best shot." The truth was I knew I would be gentle with myself, AND I would not lie (to myself and others) about my disappointment. This was new for me. I was way too accustomed to sugar-coating and moving on.

There was an inner voice that said YES, I can do this and I deserve it. Right next to it, there was a loud voice that was screaming—failure. Regardless, I had set my inten-tion and cemented it in my heart. I really wanted 100%, as I defined it—to grab the trapeze bar!

My Peak Event story continues on page 28.

My Peak Event story continues on page 28.

Remember: Be clear about your end result. Not 99% of it, all 100% of it!

Your Intention is...

Your Desire + Your Belief = Your Results

Your Desire

Everything begins with desire, consciously or not. Look around the space you are in right now. An idea as simple as a glass desk took someone's desire to make it happen. It goes something like this:

- One person says I want a curved glass table with steel legs.

- It will be a working table designed just for one person.

Next, someone sketches the design→ another person sources the parts→ a team of people assemble the parts→another team packages it to go to market → yet another team figures out how to define the audience interested in buying the table and → they pick three sales channels → one is a wholesaler, the other two are retailers→ the table is displayed at stores, in catalogs and online web sites → a customer looking for a glass table finds THIS table → she feels it's exactly what she was looking for and gets a big smile on her face →she takes that "Yes" moment into action and purchases the table → she takes it to her new office and makes it her own by adding color to the legs.

Note that the person with the original desire had very little with DOING what it takes to make the table—and yet without him it would never come to reality exactly as the table he envisioned. He expressed his **vision** and leveraged a series of other people's services to bring it to fruition.

Nothing begins without an intention, and intention begins with desire. Be it *"I will be my ideal body weight and in shape"* to *"a PC on every desk"*—there must be desire.

"When Paul Allen and I started Microsoft over 30 years ago, we had big dreams about software," recalls Gates. "We had dreams about the impact it could have. We talked about a computer on every desk and in every home. It's been amazing to see so much of that dream become a reality and touch so many lives. I never imagined what an incredible and important company would spring from those original ideas."

~ Bill Gates

Ask yourself, did the legends of innovation say "I have time to do this" or "I'll wait till someone else invents this idea I have, this desire deep inside of me." I don't think so. Every one of these legends, be it business or global leaders, attached urgency, didn't waste time and stepped forth with action—one step at a time.

Invitation 1: List your top 11 life desires, as you've imagined so far. If you cannot finish the list right away, add them as they come to you.

1.

2.

3.

4.

5.

6.

7.

8.

9.

10.

11.

Remember: NONE of us know when our last breath is scheduled. Seize your desires NOW!

Invitation 2: Which one of your deepest desires in life has already come true?

Invitation 3: How do you feel about having accomplished this desire?

Invitation 4: Start a journal. Begin my creating your "bucket list" of 101 things you want to accomplish before you die. Feel free to include the ones you've already checked off, but don't sell yourself short. If you don't complete the 101 on your first sitting, add to your list as you think of them. Don't stop at 101. Dream BIG! Copy the page and keep it in several locations—your desk, on your night stand, pasted on your bathroom mirror.

Invitation 5: Pick 3 things from your bucket list that are not yet accomplished and you deeply desire before you die. Remember, we don't know when our last breath is scheduled.

1.

2.

3.

Desire Tips

1. Be awake to your deepest desires.

2. Accept your desires without judgment.

3. Be honest, don't settle.

Your Belief

Most innovation and creation ends because the person who had the original desire did not believe it was possible. In reverse, all innovation that does come to reality is because someone really believed in the desire that it originated from.

The classic example of relentlessly believing is Thomas Edison. It took him 14 months and 1400 attempts to make the light bulb. He had 1,093 patents in his name and surely each of them had a similar journey of several attempts.

What is the biggest differentiator between legends and those that didn't achieve their desired outcome? **BELIEF!** Legends like Thomas Edison, Bill Gates, and Lance Armstrong all believed their vision was possible. These legends didn't let the "it can't be done" voices get in the way, in fact they likely ignored them vehemently. The more you focus on a belief, the stronger it grows. Naturally, they put intellect and practice into achieving their end outcome. And yet, without their relentless belief, and surrounding themselves with people who believed in their ideas and in them, they would not have succeeded.

The more we believe something is impossible, the more it will be. In business and life, we can easily get skeptical and think there are so many obstacles to achieving our intentions. Yes, most obstacles FEEL real at the time, but many have overcome those odds by simply believing they CAN. Trial and error is almost always part of the journey. Few products become successful instantly, even though it might appear that way to the end-user.

"I have missed more than 9000 shots in my career. I have lost almost 300 games. On 26 occasions I have been entrusted to take the game winning shot... and missed. And I have failed over and over and over again in my life. And that is why I succeed."

~ Michael Jordan

Remember: Have a clear vision of your intention. What you <u>*believe*</u> *will be created, like it or not.*

Invitation 6: What would you say are your beliefs, positive and negative, about success? Quickly write down what comes to you first. Don't think about it.

Positive Beliefs about Success	Negative Beliefs about Success
1.	1.
2.	2.
3.	3.
4.	4.
5.	5.

Invitation 7: Look back at your negative beliefs about success as they relate to your desire in Invitation 5 and honestly answer:

Which beliefs are keeping me from having these desires become reality? (e.g. don't have the time/money, first something else must happen)

Invitation 8: Can you let go of these beliefs?

               Yes   No

Invitation 9: Can you let go of these beliefs right now?

               Yes   No

If yes: let go of the negative belief.
If no: what will it take for you to be ready to let go of the negative beliefs?

Invitation 10: Write what you just learned about yourself in doing this exercise: your first thoughts, how these beliefs show up (or not) in your life. What's their impact on you?

Belief Tips

1. Listen to your inner voices.

2. Be aware of what you choose to believe.

3. Be open to believing anything is possible.

Your Result

We live in a results-oriented world. That is why the importance placed on a Do → Have → Be approach is the dominant state of being for many. The intention of focusing on results is 100% accurate. Yes, setting goals is great and important. And ask yourself <u>why</u> you are seeking the results you seek. In today's fast-paced world, few stop to ask why they are doing what they are doing. Once we are clear on the "why," the "what" and "how" unfold. Without a clear "why," we lack focus and often are not satisfied with the outcome.

"If your why doesn't make you cry, it's not big enough."

Here's a brief part of my friend Bryce James's story:

> *Bryce had a paragliding accident in 1995. He burst his spine allowing spinal fluid to leak internally. Laying bedridden his outlook on life was dismal. He chose not to believe in a life as a paraplegic and instead believe he can be healed. He says, "I believed at my core that I would regain feeling below the waist."*
>
> *The tipping point came a half year after the accident. "My previous girlfriend came in while I was in a typical light sleep mode and placed her head on my chest. I felt the love of her energy zoom through my body down to the big toe, the one I had been staring at for months; I sensed it had moved."*
>
> *That was the beginning of his healing. Today, at age 50, Bryce coaches freestyle skiing and plays soccer regularly. "I still have numbness in the back of my legs and feet, but I continue to improve. Do more than dream, believe in the impossible and participate in the moment at all times."*

Bryce chose to believe the impossible was possible. He also studied rigorously and tried a plethora of ways to heal himself, all primarily by focusing on his thoughts. Now he applies the same learning to continually grow deeper into understanding himself and his purpose in this life. His business practice is focused on alternative monetary systems for a better world for all people. Bryce embodies **The 101% You**, and fills me with inspiration.

<u>*Remember:*</u> *You don't have to go through the hell that Bryce did to achieve the results you desire.*

Invitation 11: Think of a time when you lived the formula and achieved a desire you believed was impossible to accomplish.

Your Desire + Your Belief = Your Results

Now, break down the elements of how you lived this formula:

Invitation 12: What did you desire?

Invitation 13: What were your beliefs before and during the journey to your result?

Invitation 14: Assuming you were satisfied with your result, what did you learn about desire and your beliefs from this event?

Result Tips

1. *Be focused on your desired outcome.*

2. *Let go of the attachment to the outcome.*

3. *Give it time to grow and stay persistent.*

Your Blockers

Finally, it is important to recognize that your core beliefs can make or break the formula of getting what you want. They can be the blockers to your success. Our core beliefs are the "programs" that are locked in our subconscious mind at a very early age. They drive your choices without you even being aware of them. Here are a few examples:

- You have to work hard to succeed

- Money doesn't grow on trees

- Only extroverts get people's attention

Research shows us that 85% of our beliefs are locked into our subconscious mind by the time we turn eight years old. Another 10% is complete by age eighteen. That only leaves 5% for our adult years. The key to unlocking these programs begins with **awareness**. When you are aware of your "hard-wired" programs, you can make different choices.

How you do anything is how you do everything.

It's your choice. First, are you willing to take a look at those programs that drive your actions? These core beliefs are what give you a sense of what's right or wrong, what's success or failure, and your purpose for being. It is only with the awareness of these programs and how they drive your life that you can CHOOSE how to RESPOND, instead of REACT to any and all events around you.

We all have positive beliefs that serve us and negative beliefs that don't. The challenge becomes recognizing whether the beliefs that drive your choices are positive or negative. Once recognized, you can make different choices next time. The current moment can never be taken back. Like it or not, it has passed and will never be repeated.

The sooner we choose to recognize the positive and negative beliefs, the faster we get to having the life we desire. Ignoring those negative beliefs (with or without awareness of them) only perpetuates more of that thinking, which results in the same results.

Remember: Know your blockers. Switch them constantly to the positive results you desire.

Invitation 15: Back in Invitation 6 you were invited to list your positive and negative beliefs about success. Since you have been reading and reflecting on these topics, have you identified any additional negative success beliefs that hold you back? Record here or use your journal if necessary.

Invitation 16: Do these negative beliefs serve a purpose? For each belief, answer these questions:

1. Yes, this belief serves a positive purpose for me.

2. This belief serves me in some ways, but not all.

3. No, this belief does not serve positive purpose for me.

Invitation 17: Now, for each negative belief, write the positive version of it on a separate page in your journal. For example, if one of your blocks is "lucky people get all the breaks," replace it with "I am attracting everything I need for this situation right now."

Blockers Tips

1. Be aware of your blockers.

2. Choose to turn blockers to positives.

3. Stay vigilant to the blocker voices.

"An ounce of performance

is worth pounds of promises."

Mae West

CHAPTER 2

STEP 2: YOUR CHOICE

MAKE SURE YOUR INTENTION IS YOUR CHOICE

My Peak Event story continued...

Step 2 of the pole exercise was to declare to the event moderator that "I, Bobby Bak-shi, choose to do this event." It was my choice.

I was clear standing at the base of the pole that this exercise was for me. It wasn't to prove anything to anyone else—my wife, my parents, my friends at home or those on my team supporting me. This realization in itself was liberating at the time, but also built great fear in me. So if I'm not being measured by anyone, who am I accountable to? Me! Yes, that was the moment of great fear, as I recognized that I am my own big-gest critic. I knew that if I didn't achieve my intention, I would be very disappointed.

I remembered too many times in life when my gut said one thing and I would still seek the advice and feedback of others to "decide" how to proceed. Now, standing at the base of the 50-foot telephone pole I knew this was a moment of great clar-ity. **I choose to do this event.** *I wasn't being asked to do it by anyone else. I had no agreement with another about the "if this" (e.g. get good grades), "then that" (e.g. reward). I was determined to prove to myself—*

I can do this!

My Peak Event story continues on page 38.

Choice Just Is

We are always at CHOICE about what state of being we will live from (how we are showing up), regardless of what is going on around us.

The best thing about choice is that it can be simple. Contrary to what many people believe, you don't need data to make a choice. You don't need to explain "why?" to someone else or even yourself. You don't need to evaluate the pros and cons. You don't need someone to validate or approve your choice. You don't need any historical data or experience to base it on. It is simply YOUR choice. In fact, if any of those things are involved—needing data, needing to evaluate pros and cons, needing input or validation from others—then you are dealing with a decision, not a choice. Choice just is!

Each moment is made up of a series of choices:

- Do you choose to wake up to your alarm or hit the snooze button?

- Do you choose to be angry at the driver that cuts you off or just let it go?

- Do you choose to follow traffic laws or not?

Our cumulative choices affect our view of our own selves. Are you aware of the choices you are making, choice after choice after choice?

Your choices impact not only you but others as well. It is up to you to discern if you care about the impact on yourself or others. Here are a few examples of the impact your choices have on yourself and others:

- You can choose to be angry at someone. That's your choice. However, you have no control over how that person responds (or reacts) to your anger.

Remember: Your Choice is…**your** choice.

- You can choose to roll through a stop sign and take a chance. That's your choice. However, you have no control if a police officer is present and gives you a ticket.

- You can choose to stay unhappily in a relationship. That's your choice. However, you have no control over the other person's choices.

Because it's simply your choice, you do not need data to substantiate your choice. However, recognize there are always consequences for actions we take, including our thoughts. We are all continuously choosing, either consciously or subconsciously. You do not need data or past experiences to substantiate your choices. You get to decide what's right/wrong for you, despite the consequences that might come from the choices and actions you take.

Invitation 18: List 11 choices you made in the last day. Remember, there are no right/wrong choices or big/small choices. They are simply events that have occurred. Feel free to write in your journal if you want to keep the specific items private. Simply write down the first things that come to your mind.

1.

2.

3.

4.

5.

6.

7.

8.

9.

10.

11.

Invitation 19: Now, looking at the cumulative sample of 11 choices you made yesterday, how do you feel about your pattern of making choices?

5   Totally satisfied with my choices

4   Somewhat satisfied with my choices

3   Neither satisfied nor dissatisfied with my choices

2   Somewhat dissatisfied with my choices

1   Totally dissatisfied with my choices

Invitation 20: What did you learn about your pattern of making choices based on this exercise?

Choice Just Is Tips

1. Remember, you are always at choice.

2. Only YOU make choices for you.

3. Be aware of how you feel about your choices.

Own Your Choice

Great leaders own the choices they make. They might be unpopular for their choice. They may be asked to "prove it" or provide data to substantiate their choice. At this step, they need not do that. That's when data and explanation might be required.

Even though choice simply is and you don't need to justify or explain it, you do need to own how you show up in the world. Choice is the foundation of being **The 101% You**. For example, you come to work in the morning and there's an urgent project from your boss that has to get done today, on top of an already 100% packed schedule. You reprioritize the day to ensure you get the urgent project done. The difference lies in how you show up for that event, the change in your expected day. Do you choose to get angry, stressed, or do you quickly reprioritize and get engaged in that higher priority project to get it done?

It's up to you to choose, and own your choice. You are ultimately responsible to yourself first.

When you do not own your choices, you are living in victim mentality. What is victim mentality? Victim mentality means you deflect taking responsibility for your choices with thoughts like: *"it's not my fault; I'm not lucky; I never get what I deserve."* A person living in victim mentality shifts the blame for their choices to others.

Continuing to illustrate lessons from the movie "Invictus:"

> *Nelson Mandela made a choice. In the first few days of his becoming President he saw the vision of how supporting an all-white rugby team can be the illustration of true compassion, forgiveness and unity. Despite all the opposition from his closest advisors, he stuck with his choice to back this team, just the way they were. He did not interfere with the structure of the team. He didn't ask the nation to come along with him in this belief (at least not as they showed it in the movie "Invictus"). It was simply his choice to support and showcase the rugby team.*

You might think, *"But Nelson Mandela had an agenda in this choice."* Sure he did. The key lesson here is to recognize there is no "right or wrong" in a choice. It simply is. Does it move into a decision process? Not always but it might. Data can be required to bring others onboard, not for you to trust what you believe in.

Remember: You get to choose if you are happy or unhappy. It's simply your choice. No data required.

Invitation 21: How do you feel about your choices in these areas of your life? Feel free to modify the labels if they don't apply or add some of your own:

	Extremely Satisfied	Fairly Satisfied	Neither	Fairly Dissatisfied	Extremely Dissatisfied
Work you do	5	4	3	2	1
People you spend time with	5	4	3	2	1
Primary relationship	5	4	3	2	1
Self-care time	5	4	3	2	1
Food you eat	5	4	3	2	1
City you live in	5	4	3	2	1
Your home	5	4	3	2	1
...	5	4	3	2	1

Invitation 22: For those areas you scored 1 to 3, who is primarily responsible for this score?

1. One other individual

2. A group of individuals

3. An organization/company

4. Entirely me

Invitation 23: For those areas you scored 1 to 3, are you interested in changing those choices?

Yes   No

If Yes: write in your journal some ideas on how to start this change today. Ideally, construct commitments around them and ask someone you trust to support you in accountability with those commitments.

Own Your Choice Tips

1. Recognize when you do or don't own your choice.

2. Embrace the power of your choice.

3. Frequently examine how you feel about your choices.

Being Self-Responsible

In the context of being **The 101% You**, let us focus on what is in our immediate control and our invitation is to contemplate on what it means for you. Here are some of the core elements that make up being self-responsible:

1. Aware of what you are creating toward the life of your choice.

2. Conscious about your part in any event/situation.

3. Awake to your patterns, your thoughts and emotions.

4. Clear about your true desires and seeking directly to meet them.

5. Free to ask for what you want of others, knowing that you may not get it.

6. Direct, clear and concise in the way you communicate your thoughts.

7. Respectful of your physical state: what you eat, exercising and your safety.

Self-responsibility is about always staying on your side of the road/fence. Many of us find it easy to see what's wrong in others and point outward. Few point inward and learn from the patterns that show up repeatedly in their lives. Rarely do we look at situations to own our part in them.

Let's look at a simple example. *I have just put my groceries in my car and need to put the shopping cart away. I choose the easiest way to dispose of the cart and not take the time to stack it in the area that's designated to gather carts. I seek to find that quick solution, to save ME time as I am so busy.* Being self-responsible means returning the cart to the proper area.

Sometimes we make choices to place that cart precariously so even though it looks "safe" on top of the curb when we put it up there, it is likely to roll off and hit another car. Now take the reverse of this. How do you feel when you see a shopping cart "wandering" in a parking lot, obstructing a parking spot that you could be using or, even worse, rolling off that curb and dinging your car?

That self-awareness on our part in every choice is self-responsibility. No, we cannot know the consequences of our choices, yet staying awake to our part is a great start. Play this out in the workforce. How often do you find yourself (out loud or in your head) saying: *"If only my manager was clear about what she wants from me. Why doesn't senior management give us a clear vision? Why did I not get promoted?"*

Self-responsibility means asking the questions and having the conversations with your manager that need to happen.

Let's not confuse self-responsibility with being self-critical. Blame, shame and finger-pointing is a choice that goes both ways—out to people and events from us, and inward onto our self. The objective is to continuously learn and grow.

Invitation 24: Take a look at these elements of self-responsibility and evaluate yourself. Don't think about it. Check the answer that comes to you first.

	Most of the time	Sometimes	Rarely
I am aware of what I am creating toward the life I want.	3	2	1
I am conscious about my part in any event/situation	3	2	1
I am awake to my patterns, my thoughts & feelings.	3	2	1
I am clear about my true desires and seek to meet them directly.	3	2	1
I freely ask for what I want of others, knowing I may not get it.	3	2	1
I am direct, clear and concise in the way I communicate.	3	2	1
I respect my physical state by eating healthy and exercising.	3	2	1

Invitation 25: Write in your journal how you feel about this exercise. Remember, this is for your own benefit. If this brought up feelings and thoughts, write about them.

Invitation 26: Even if you marked "most of the time" in all of the above, consider something you do differently this week to experience stepping fully into your self-responsibility. For example, if you have been hesitant to suggest a change/an improvement at work, clearly state your desire to the person who can do something about it.

SELF- RESPONSIBILITY Tips

1.Be conscious to your part in any situation.

2. Discern what is and is not in your control.

3.If it's out of your control, ask for what you want.

"One worthwhile task carried to a successful conclusion is worth half-a-hundred half-finished tasks."

Malcom S. Forbes

CHAPTER 3

STEP 3:

YOUR COMMITMENT

MAKE IT REAL AND BE ACCOUNTABLE

My Peak Event story continued...

I stepped up to one of the workshop leaders, just before starting up the pole. He asked me a clear and direct question: "Bobby, what do you want from this event?" I looked him in the eyes and with all the conviction in my heart said: "I want my 100%. I want to grab that trapeze bar. Anything less is not MY 100% today." I was sick of coming so close to my prize and not getting it. Too often in life I came close, even 99%, and it wasn't my 100%.

At the time, I distinctly remember shaking with fear. The fear was about not getting MY 100%. It wasn't about falling, getting hurt, or what others would think. Luckily I was clear about that. The commitment I made was strictly made with myself. That was it! Speaking it to one of the workshop leaders simply meant I had declared it as my intention. Now I was being supported in accountability by the workshop leader to do what I said I'd do—grab that trapeze bar!

The fear was like an electric current running through my whole body. I was tense and ready. There was clearly an energy building up in me that I had not recalled experiencing before. Now I know this energy was the unification of ALL of me—my soul, my heart, my mind and my body—preparing for battle. I was stepping forth into a symbolic exercise, representing the biggest battles of my life. Despite having accomplished many great things in life, this exercise signified my Achilles' heel.

My Peak Event story continues on page 48.

Your Accountability

Effective commitment setting is a binary decision. You are either 100% IN or 100% OUT. Anything in between is simply a way to deny, suppress or hide your true desire. Be clear what you are committing to and what the expectations are, first to you and then to others involved, if necessary. Many organizations use the acronym SMART for commitment setting. Here's Resonant Insights' version of this important acronym:

Specific:	State your desired outcome in great detail.
Measureable:	You and all involved can answer a binary "yes" or "no" when done.
Actionable:	A tangible action in a format that all can measure.
Responsible:	You are responsible to all impacted that the action will be completed.
Timely:	A specific date and time by when it will be done.

A lot of our commitments stay in our head. For instance, how often do we say I want to be my ideal weight or I want to save money? Have the courage to speak your clear intention to another. A clear and concise commitment may feel uncomfortable at first—try it and see how liberating and empowering it is.

It may look like this:

Specific:	I will weigh my ideal weight of _____ pounds/KGs
Measureable:	I will record my weight daily
Actionable:	I will exercise for an hour, 4 times a week (add details)
Responsible:	I will report progress to my accountability buddy by 5pm every Friday
Timely:	I will achieve my intention by _____ (date)

Remember: All commitments/contracts are re-negotiable but ONLY if you do it prior to the deadline.

No one can "hold" you accountable. Being accountable is up to you. Others can simply SUPPORT you in accountability. In business, this usually shows up as tangible sub-agreements—deadlines, specific things you have to deliver, etc. The more control you have over designing those agreements and feeling they are congruent with your desires, the more likely you are to get them done. In the end, both you and those you are serving win.

As you are always at choice, you may also renegotiate your commitments in advance, meaning sufficiently before the deadline. Naturally, you can only ask; it is up to the other person to accept, reject or make a counter offer/perspective for you to consider.

Invitation 27: We all make commitments in all areas of our lives. This exercise is an opportunity to recognize where you are making commitments consciously vs. subconsciously. Answer each of these starting with *"I am clear about..."*

	My commitments		My Choices		My SMART commitments	
With myself	Yes	No	Yes	No	Yes	No
With my manager	Yes	No	Yes	No	Yes	No
With my co-workers	Yes	No	Yes	No	Yes	No
With my primary partner	Yes	No	Yes	No	Yes	No
With my family	Yes	No	Yes	No	Yes	No
With my communities	Yes	No	Yes	No	Yes	No

Remember, all these invitations are simply designed to raise your self-awareness. Ponder on your answers and determine what you've learned about yourself and if you choose to change anything in your life or not.

Invitation 28: Take some time to write down at least one area of your life where you choose to construct commitments differently and what that would look like.

Accountability Tips

1.Be clear WHY you commit.

2. Be conscious WHAT you commit to.

3.Apply SMART to commitments you choose.

Your Witnesses

A witness, in the context of these steps, is a person who believes you can accomplish what you commit to. They believe you are capable. They have nothing vested in the result and are not judging you one way or the other. YOU must be the one who invites this person to support you in accountability. For many of us, when we speak our intention to another person we respect and apply the SMART way of doing it. This adds the urgency to getting things done. In the beginning, we all intend to give most things our 100% best. But do you have someone who reminds you about the exact intention and the specific commitments that go with it? It helps to have a witness who will ask these questions to support you:

1. What will you do?

2. By when will you do it?

3. How will I know?

Make sure to pick someone you totally trust to be your witness. Be careful who you invite to this agreement as they are your support in knowing that you can accomplish this and more. They believe (bear witness) you have **The 101% You** that is needed to make anything shift from the impossible to the possible. If you sense even a bit of negative belief in them toward the commitment, cancel that invitation and start over.

Think of this concept as akin to people who "have your back." They are people who want you to succeed. They are your cheerleaders and champion you to success. They don't mentor you with the "how" and "what," they simply believe in your "why," your purpose.

You may not have a choice in who you make a commitment with and are accountable to (e.g. your job requires you to agree to commitments with your manager). However, you get to choose who can be your witness, who can support you, in meeting your commitments.

Asking someone to be a witness for you may mean that you are opening yourself up to another person in a way that you have not before. It can be scary, and it will likely deepen your relationship with that person if you choose to ask.

Remember: Others can support you in accountability; they can't "make" you accountable. Even at work!

Invitation 29: Do you presently apply this concept of having an explicit, SMART agreement with someone who supports you in meeting the commitments you make to yourself and others?

        Yes   No

Invitation 30: If yes, how many such people support you/witness you in meeting your commitments?

Just one person	1
Two to three people	2
Four to five people	3
Five to ten people	4
More than 10 people	5

Invitation 31: If no, <u>are you willing</u> to invite people to support you in meeting your commitments, recognizing that no one can make you accountable?

        Yes   No

Invitation 32: If yes, <u>will you</u> invite people to support you in meeting your commitments, in all areas of your life?

        Yes   No

Invitation 33: Write down here or in your journal what you learned about yourself from this exercise.

Your Witness Tips

1. No one can hold you accountable; they can only support you in accountability.

2. Identify people you trust to witness and support your commitments.

3. Be conscious of your commitments: who, why, how, what and when.

Regret-Free Commitments

Since life is simply a series of choices and commitments:

Regret-Free Commitments = a Regret-Free LIFE!

Regret-free commitments mean stepping up and committing to those things that you truly want in your life now — today!

How often have you regretted any of the following type of events?

- I wish I had said something during that meeting.

- I wish I had introduced myself to that beautiful person in the elevator.

- I wish I had put my hat in the ring for that exciting project.

- I wish I had more time with my kids.

- I wish I had learned to play the guitar.

- _____

- _____

Make sure to fill in your own. You know them right away. They are usually sitting in your subconscious mind waiting to be "invited" to being reconsidered. Remember, you are always at choice. What's stopping you from making different choices right now? Simply OTHER commitments you are choosing to make more important and the limiting beliefs, the blockers to living **The 101% You**.

We all lead very busy lives in this modern age. Regardless of your marital status, whether or not you have kids, the number of hours you work—I've almost never heard someone say: "I have all the time in the world, what should I do with it?" The bigger question is: are you conscious of HOW you are spending your time and is it in alignment with what you truly want to commit to for the life you desire?

Remember: Be clear if you have any regrets and consciously choose what to do or not to do about them.

What do you choose to make more important in your life? Why do you deny, hide or suppress those deep desires that would make you smile and jump with joy? What promises have you made yourself that you have broken time and time again or, worse yet, totally given up on? Stop settling for "good enough," go for YOUR best life ever and know that your past is not the indicator of your now and future. You create your life, with every commitment you make.

Invitation 34: Honestly ask yourself, if you were to die RIGHT NOW as you are reading this, would you say you have no regrets in your life? Totally 100% regret-free?

Yes   No

Invitation 35: **If Yes**, congratulations! May you continue to live the life you dreamed. Take time to write a few events that came up as you did this and share them with those you trust.

Invitation 36: **If no**, congratulations! You have the opportunity to make those commitments that get you closer to a regret-free life. First, take time to acknowledge those events in your life where you have no regrets—the things you are most proud of.

Invitation 37: **If no**: Now jot down those regrets that you <u>could</u> create new commitments to change and have the life you desire.

Invitation 38: Are you willing to make new commitments to have 100% of the life you desire? If yes, start writing in your journal and put it all down. Add to your Bucket List and more.

Yes   No

Regret-Free Tips

1. Be aware of your regrets.

2. Choose the regrets you wish to do something about.

3. Let go of the regrets you choose to leave behind.

Falling Short

Despite your best intentions, there will still be times when you don't meet your expectations 100%. You fall short on your commitment. What do you do? Many of us brood about it, to ourselves or others. We retreat into a place of disappointment and "impossible" again. The worst outcome is to believe that not meeting your 100% is failure and not try to attempt it again.

Falling short of your stated 100% is simply an opportunity to redo it, consciously. First, feel your true disappointment and celebrate how far you have come compared to if you did not try at all. Next, remember it's all about practice, practice, practice. Go ahead and give yourself permission to try again, always believing you can do it and that it's possible to break through the barriers.

Keep a focus on your desired outcome. The more you think about it and visualize what it would feel like when you have it, the more you will attract it to becoming real. Every time those thoughts of disbelief pop up, simply hit the "I CAN" button. Make the flip and focus on your desired outcome.

Make sure not to interpret this as "it will happen in time." The doing will happen and must follow to move forward in action. The key is to examine the beliefs, the patterns underneath the feeling of falling short. A baby doesn't know that feeling. What limiting patterns, if any, did you take in from your environment very early on that drive your choices?

Let me illustrate with my experience of participating in group sports:

> I was never good at group sports of any kind. I never chose to step up, participate and practice. When I did try to play as a little boy, I was ashamed for not being good at it. Only recently, as a new member of our local YMCA, I have chosen to start and end my workouts with shooting a few hoops. I always set myself an intention. On most days I am looking to make at least three baskets. I stay and practice until I do it. The time it takes me to achieve that intention is getting shorter and shorter.

Does this pattern show up in my life outside of sports? Absolutely! Be aware of those patterns, the voices that allow you to fall short in any part of your life.

Remember: Practice. Practice. Practice. Never give up on those deep desires. Celebrate your progress.

Invitation 39: Do you feel you have fallen short in any area of your life?

     Yes   No

Invitation 40: Are you willing to give yourself an opportunity to redo things, for yourself?

     Yes   No

Invitation 41: Describe what that would look like, using the SMART commitment approach:

Specific: What is your specific desired outcome?

Measureable: Can it be measured by all involved?
     Yes   No

(Detail how you will measure it)

Actionable: What is the tangible action in a format that all can measure?

Responsible: Are you willing to take full responsibility for this commitment?

     Yes   No

Timely: When will it be done? (Date) _____

Invitation 42: Who will you invite to support you with accountability? Make sure they accept your invitation and agree to support your SMART commitments.

Falling Short Tips

1.Be true to yourself when you feel you fall short.

2. Check what beliefs are underneath this feeling of falling short.

3. Be open to welcoming that YOU CAN accomplish this, if you choose.

CHAPTER 4

STEP 4:

YOUR WORK

APPROACH YOUR INTENTIONS WITH FOCUS AND TENACITY

My Peak Event story continued...

I started climbing the telephone pole, grabbing one metal staple at a time, deliber-ately and nervously. My palms were sweating. My boots felt like they were slipping off the metal staples. At the same time I had fear that I would let go and fall. I knew I had a team supporting me below. I was connected to them with ropes—they were billeting for me. I knew they had my back. It was the fear of ending my experience way too soon and not getting my 100% that had me anxious. I was totally focused on the climb, taking my time and not rushing it.

At one point I had this deep desire to look down to see how far I had come. Not a great idea. I momentarily panicked. I decided at that moment to not look down (back) and stay 100% focused on what was ahead, the next step. It worked.

As I got closer to the top, but still a few staples from the pizza-sized platform, I froze. I was completely panicking from within. I felt like a volcano was starting to grumble from within me. I made sure my feet were planted strong on the staples below me. I could not move. I was shaking from the core.

My body got tight. My hands gripped the staples hard, as blisters developed. The overwhelming voice that came out as the volcano within started to rumble was "I can do this." It started soft and only to myself. I kept repeating it as a chant: "I can, I can, I can, I can, I can," fighting the voice of "I can't, I can't, I can't." My internal "I can" chant became louder to me. I started to look up at the small platform I was about to get on top of, again paralyzed with the enormity of how the heck I would get on top of that little thing. At some point, the "I can't" voice got drowned by the "I can" and the volcano starting to erupt.

My Peak Event story continues on page 60.

What's Yours to Do

When I was climbing the pole, I was 100% clear about my desired outcome, even though I didn't necessarily know "how" to do the next step. All I had to do was WEL-COME what was in front of me to do next. What I focused on was my intention. My intention that day was crystal clear: I wanted to grab the trapeze bar. Oh yeah, by the way, that meant I had to get on top of the 50-foot telephone pole, balance on top of a tiny platform, then turn my entire body around on the platform and leap for the trapeze bar—not falling and losing my end prize. That was my chosen intention for that event.

Do all people know what's theirs to do, what their purpose in life is? Your purpose in life, that big question of *"why am I here?"* is what we focus on at Resonant Insights. We believe all of us know our purpose deep inside of us. Many of us take on what our society and environment has taught us to believe as our work, our purpose. We latch on to roles and titles: "I am a Dad so I must...," "I am a female executive so I am expected to...," "I am a teacher so my students expect..." When you go deep enough under the surface of all those roles, there is always a deeper desire, a calling that is waiting to be fulfilled. At Resonant Insights we ask the deep questions to evoke the truth of who you are. This is where "what's yours to do" resides.

Regardless of whether you believe you are clear about your purpose, I encourage you to continue with the workbook and see where you come out at the end. Consistent with the concept of 100%—what's yours to do, only you can do. If you don't rise up to your life purpose, it simply won't get done. It won't get done the way you would create it. Think about it: would we have PCs and Macs the way we do today if Bill Gates and Steve Jobs didn't invent them? That is very unlikely. Would we have something like a PC/Mac? Maybe, but it wouldn't be the same thing.

Out of the billions of human beings on earth, only YOU can do what you do EXACTLY the way you do it. Yes, the outcome may look very similar but there's a unique stamp we all put on our way of doing something.

In the Introduction, we quote Michael Jordan listing his failures. Michael is a classic example of living at 101%, often full of the Power of Inspiration. Were there times he didn't do so well on the court? Absolutely! What really matters? He was clear about his 100% best at any given moment. He was in his element, and living his purpose as a master of basketball.

Who decides what your work is? YOU do. Sure you have commitments to others. When you come from a place of Intention → Choice → Commitment your actions provide contentment with your decision to make something happen.

Remember: Your work is your purpose. Not the "job" you do but the gifts you give and the legacy you leave.

Invitation 43: Are you clear about "your work" in this life (not your job)?

Yes   No

Invitation 44: If no, are you keen to explore more deeply what your work is or is not?

Yes   No (come back if you change your mind)

Invitation 45: If yes, here are some statements to fill out to get you started:

I feel strongly about changing…

I want my life to be more…

My core values are most real to me when I am…

I feel my best when…

My biggest desire is to live my life…

Invitation 46: Now, based on your answers above and anything else you wish to draw from, give yourself permission to create your life purpose. Remember, you can change it.

(For example, here is mine: *"I empower a world of compassion, courage and abundance by inspiring people to be their best."*)

What's Yours To Do Tips

1. Be clear about what your "work" is.

2. Examine WHY you do what you do.

3. Recognize and celebrate your uniqueness.

You spot it, you got it.

Like it or not, when you see, feel or think something about another person or a situation it is because you see it in yourself. We can only recognize what we see in ourselves or what we are familiar with. When we pay attention to something or someone it is because we resonate with it—good or bad. For instance, when we admire a leader for particular qualities it is because we emulate those qualities in ourselves. In the negative, when we criticize or condemn someone or something it is because we recognize that quality in ourselves. It's familiar territory for us, consciously or subconsciously, to attach relevance with other experiences in our memory.

Our unconscious brain is our true power center. Did you know that 17% of our total brain mass is conscious, yet it controls only 2-4% of our actual perceptions and behaviors? What impact do you think this has on how you view the world?

Everyone and everything around us is an opportunity to reflect on ourselves. They are simply holding up a mirror for us to see our own self in the person or situation that we pay attention to, be it positive or negative.

Most of us do not take the time to pay attention to WHAT we are paying attention to. Even fewer examine WHY we are paying attention to someone or something, we simply do it. We get sucked into the energy of that person or situation like a black-hole and go straight to connecting it with patterns in our memory. Let me illustrate with my own example:

Until recently, I expected people to show up on time for scheduled appointments because I pride myself on being on time and usually early. I would judge and resent people who would not show up on time or take a specific time commitment seriously.

This pattern repeated itself often with various people. I was in such a strong place of righteous indignation that I lost sight of what my role was. At the same time, I had the realization that this recurring pattern was about ME and not them; it wasn't about their not showing up on time, but it was more about them not showing up for me. I took it personally. With that awareness I could laugh and let that go. Further, I was able to see that I was not showing up for others, in other ways. Not necessarily in regard to timeliness but for instance not listening attentively and giving them my 100%. I concluded that this mirror of people around my tardiness pet peeve was simply a lesson for me to go deeper and learn more about myself. I now show up more fully in all areas of my life that matter to me, thanks to this deeper understanding of myself.

Remember: We are all mirrors for each other.

Invitation 47: Do you see the good and bad in others as a MIRROR OF YOU or do you disagree with this concept? Write in your journal about how you feel about it.

5   Totally see it and agree with the concept

4   Somewhat see it and agree with it

3   Indifferent

2   Don't really see it and somewhat disagree with it

1   Do not see it and disagree with it

Invitation 48: Pick a pet peeve that bugs you in other people. Write it down in your journal every time you see the pattern occur and rate it with intensity as follows:

3   Really bothered by it and had strong emotions around it

2   Not that bothered but still impacted by it

1   Recognized the pattern and am able to let go of it quickly

Invitation 49: At the end of the week, look back at your patterns and their frequency. What have you learned about yourself? And what do you choose to change or do differently so you can release this pattern, if anything?

You Spot It, You Got It Tips

1. Recognize the mirror others are for you.

2. Be aware of your pattern you see in others.

3. Recognize your pet peeves are about you.

Grow or Decay

Everything has its season and so does every choice we make in life. A choice at this moment that feels great may not feel that great a bit later. What do you do when that happens? Most of us make a different choice. You can choose to look back at all your choices as generative (taking you forward) or decaying (setting you back or keeping you stagnant). Regardless of whether you are conscious about it or not, you are always making choices that either generate growth or increase decay.

It is as simple as our body. Actually, let's narrow it down to a toothache. Most of us have had one at some point in life. That pain, usually localized to a tooth, is a sure sign of decay. What do you do? You go to the dentist. The dentist takes a look and gives you a recommendation based on data/information. You then choose to say "yes" or "no" to that recommended path. Despite the data, it's your choice. If you don't like the recommendation, maybe you seek another opinion before making your choice. In the end, you likely choose to fix the tooth and stop the pain. You take generative action. You move forward. You do what is right for you to do at the time, until the next point at which you need to make the choice to grow or decay.

Your Peak Event is likely a clear example of a time when you were 100% focused on growth. Change is not easy for most of us. It's when we embrace it and lean into the discomfort that we break through into new ground. When you are faced with those challenges, recalling your Peak Event can be an invaluable tool to give you comfort and support.

Remember: Be aware of what in your life is growing and thriving vs. decaying or dormant.

Invitation 50: What is the current state of the following areas of your life? Feel free to add your own areas if you choose. Remember: growth means the quality of that area for You! Yes, we deliberately left out an "out," such as "it depends" or "in the middle." Time doesn't stop until it's over for us. In the meantime, our choices are constant.

Life Area	Growing	Decaying
Primary relationship		
Family ties		
Friendships		
Financial freedom		
Career path		
Creative expression		
Physical well-being		
Daily level of energy		
Nutrition to your body		
Spiritual connection		
Home/physical space		
Connection with nature		
...		
...		

Invitation 51: For areas you checked "decaying," write at least one SMART commitment in your journal to flip it to growth in the next 30 days. Share these commitments with a person you trust and ask for support accountability (e.g. I will take time for myself).

As with all these exercises, be gentle with yourself. Commitments can be small steps toward having the life you choose. Give yourself permission to select the commitments you choose.

Invitation 52: For areas checked "growing," write at least one SMART commitment in your journal to grow it even further in the next 30 days. Share these commitments with a person you trust and ask for support accountability (e.g. spend more quality time with my loved ones).

Grow or Decay Tips

1. Evaluate your choices as generative or decaying.

2. Remind yourself of your Peak Event when faced with a challenge.

3. Keep your focus on your intention to pull you forward.

FOCUS One Step at a Time

When I was climbing the 50-foot telephone pole, and because I wanted my intention to manifest, I only had one choice—to stay focused on what was immediately in front of me. The whole concept of "being in the now" is actually about being both mindfully focused on what you are doing in the present moment while aiming for a future event. Without a target, we are floundering in nothingness.

Let me illustrate with the example of a pilot of an airplane. We take flying so much for granted today and most of us don't think twice about take-off and landing, except when there's a delay, a rough flight or other "unusual circumstances." Here's what I believe happens in a cockpit:

The pilot of an airplane must be constantly present to what is happening at the present moment. She is checking the many controls that let her know the present conditions of the airplanes' flight path. There is a lot happening. She is usually supported by a co-pilot and maybe another officer. They each have specific duties. Eventually they are all focused on a future event—landing the plane safely at a particular destination, right down to the specific runway they will land on. Along the way, there are many opportunities for the pilot to determine how to proceed. For instance, a change in the weather might warrant changing the altitude of the plane. This requires taking several steps that will yield a desired result. There's always a constant adjustment until the conditions are just right to put things on "cruise control" for some time AND the pilot cannot walk away from the situation without assigning tasks to his skilled team in the cockpit. Without staying present to BOTH the present moment and the future desired end outcome, no flight can be successful.

That's the power of focus. It does not have to be dramatic as in the story of my Peak Event of climbing of a fifty-foot pole or Your Peak Event. Focus is necessary in all areas of life—from the time you pull your car onto the road, to being totally present in a meeting at work and back to being home and present with the family. Without focus, we lack clarity of purpose. Without clarity of purpose, we lack a target to go after—an end outcome, a result.

A pilot's "purpose" is generative—to take her passengers from Point A to Point B. However, there are many choices that are degenerative. Most planes and their pilots are using autopilot these days. When done consciously this is generative and focused. When used with less than 100% focus that same autopilot can become degenerative; human error is usually a major factor in most airplane accidents. When do You go into autopilot? Does it serve you? How does it serve you? Being aware of what you are focused on is the start to choosing growth or decay in all areas of your life. When you are in control, you get to choose what you focus on.

Remember: Human beings are results oriented. Be conscious to what you choose to focus on creating.

Invitation 53: List three activities in your life right now where you desire more focus. Think of things that you desire and have postponed, not made time for, or had hesitation to tackle.

1.

2.

3.

Invitation 54: Now, think of a time when you had 100% focus. Describe that event:

Invitation 55: Based on your experience in the event above, what are 5 lessons you learned about yourself that you can apply to the three activities where you desire more focus?

1.

2.

3.

4.

5.

FOCUS One Step At A Time Tips

1. Decide what's important to focus on.

2. Determine what's stopping you.

3. Create a commitment plan to get it done.

"Not everything that can be counted counts.

And not everything that counts

can be counted."

Albert Einstein

CHAPTER 5

STEP 5:

YOUR POWER

LOOK YOUR FEARS IN THE EYES AND DO IT ANYWAY

My Peak Event story continued...

There I was, with my nose right under the pizza-sized platform. That was the top of the pole and I knew this was the moment I feared the most. My brain was firing all these signals of how to get on top based on what I had observed others do. There were many ways to do it and, deep inside me, I knew there was just one way for me to get on top—to just do it! (A tip of the hat to Nike).

It was time. I knew I had to do it, regardless of whether I felt ready or not. That chant of "I can" was now constant and it got louder. My jaw was tight. My face was full of determined desire. I knew I wanted this prize and I had to muster up every bit of energy to get on top of that tiny platform. The volcano fully erupted and I let out the most guttural scream I can ever recall myself releasing. I was in full battle mode and on autopilot toward my goal. I took one hand and put it on the platform. I then put my other hand on the other side of the platform. I pushed hard as I screamed louder and the volcano fully erupted.

I propelled myself onto the platform in one big and determined push. There I was, standing on top of the pole and shaking violently. The roaring scream stopped and an instant "oh shit" feeling started to bubble up. The pole was shaking. My legs were wobbling. The panic of falling and ending my experience, not getting my prize, were firing in me.

My Peak Event story continues on page 74.

Courageous or Complacent

It took courage for Gandhi to stay the course with what he believed in. It took Martin Luther King courage to achieve greater freedom for African Americans than before. It took courage and tenacity for Thomas Edison to try endlessly before inventing the light bulb. It took courage for Lance Armstrong to enter and win the Tour de France after his battle with cancer. It took Oprah courage along the many ups and downs of her career to create her current media empire. It took courage for Donald Trump to come back strong from bankruptcy.

Yes, these are examples of legends, but that's not the point. If you desire to grow and not decay, there are times when you must muster up the courage to face your fears and move THROUGH them. In order to live the 101% best you there is, ask yourself:

Do you have the courage to be all of who you are meant to be?

You can settle for the comfortable, the tried, the tested, the norm, the status quo, and the accepted and be complacent. That's totally your choice. Maybe you are afraid to "rock the boat" by standing up for what you believe in. Maybe you are concerned about people pointing at you and saying *"who the heck do you think you are?"* Only you are the judge of you. Maybe you are satisfied with being "good enough." That works for many. Remember, there's no right or wrong. However, good enough doesn't typically move you from where you are today to where you desire to be. It takes courage to push through those blockers and have the life YOU choose to have. It's simple but not always easy to have the life of your choice.

You get to decide if you live a life full of regrets, full of numbing out things that are unpleasant, full of giving up, or as I call it, being a meek mouse. Imagine instead that you muster up all your courage and fiercely lean into the roar of what frightens you the most and burst through those barriers to realize they were simply in your imagination, the same imagination that can steer you toward generating the life of your choice.

Invitation 56: Now recall one of your Peak Events. You likely had fear before accomplishing that outcome. Describe how you can apply the same energy that triggered that outcome toward this desire that you are unable to create?

Invitation 57: Give your courageous self a name. Get creative. It could be an animal, a movie or other fictional character, a super hero, etc. The key is that YOU relate to that name. When you are sitting in fear and not ready to move forward, tap into the energy of your courage by recalling this name. Step fully into "playing" this courageous self that this name represents.

Courageous Tips

1. Be aware of the feelings you are denying yourself.

2. Choose to walk through your fears courageously.

3. Start with small things to test the waters.

Trust Your Gut

There are many practices to live a balanced life of mind, body and soul. Few of these practices teach us how to trust our gut instinct. Remember, we are primal beings. Fear is a necessary mechanism to know when to fight or flight. Today, most of us are "domesticated" enough not to physically fight, however most of us are fighting an internal battle all day, and all night: against our thoughts and what we make up about the world around us. That fight or flight instinct comes primarily from our gut, our knowing self, as opposed to our thinking or feeling self.

My Peak Event was a pivotal metaphor of my life because I chose to make it so. Something deep inside of me placed great importance to the event of climbing a pole and catching a trapeze bar. An inner voice said: "prove it to yourself." Out of the many lessons that are packed in this metaphor, trusting my gut is the core of it all. My brain said I wanted it. My heart desired it. It was my gut that said: "YES. We can do this." My gut instincts were so awake and focused that I did not even recognize how strongly I was operating from that place as I did the steps of the pole exercise. I only later realized they were what propelled me forward.

Trusting your gut goes hand-in-hand with believing in yourself or whatever you set out to accomplish. Practicing and accepting this part of you is critical in order to overcome the challenges and voices of "it's impossible or cannot be done" that will likely be coming up from you or from others to you. First YOU need to be convinced it CAN BE DONE in order to fuel the actions that will make it so.

The best way to know you can trust your gut, and trust yourself, is to tap into Your Peak Events. Remind yourself of those times when you thought something was impossible to accomplish. Break it down with the Seven Steps and see how your choices had you operating from your gut. The following exercises will walk you through this.

Know your Gut. Feel Your Power

Remember: Examine those voices of "should" and check your gut on what's yours to do.

Invitation 58: How would you evaluate yourself in trusting your gut in these areas of your life? Think of specific actions you've taken and consider if your gut had a primary, secondary, or no role at all to play in your gut vs. your mind and/or your heart?

	Primary role	Secondary role	No role at all
Ideal job			
Current job			
Your primary relationship			
Friends to hang out with			
Food choices			
Entertainment choices			
...			

Invitation 59: Are you interested in becoming more aware of your gut instincts and seeing how you feel about them?

Yes   No

Invitation 60: If yes, take at least one event or choice you made today and journal to what extent it involved trusting your gut vs. your mind or your heart.

Trusting Your Gut Tips

1. Listen for your inner voices.

2. Be aware if you accept or deny your gut.

3. Trust your gut instincts.

Define Power for You

Probably more taboo than talking about money, race, and politics is talking about power. I mean TRULY talking about it. Ask yourself, have you had a deep conversation with someone about how you define power? This is a critical place to start in being self-empowered.

The word "power" has been associated with a lot of misunderstanding and is plagued with negative connotations. We get caught up in how abuse of power by leaders makes it a bad word. Remember, just as Hitler used power to destroy, Gandhi used it to unite and serve.

As with nature, every element has a positive and a negative. The wind, water and earth are critical to our sustenance, and yet they can also destroy us. We know that because we have tangible facts, evidence to show how that same pleasant ocean beach we enjoy can also sweep thousands instantly to their death in a tsunami.

In the end, only YOU can define what power means to you. Like everything, it's your choice. If you think otherwise, you are allowing the outside environment to influence your reality. Then you have given away your power and are living in victim mentality. For a refresher on victim mentality, visit the earlier lesson on 'Own Your Choice.'

A common myth, and excuse for not living your power 100%, is that if one person is "powerful" others must be weak. All of us can stand in our own power. Let the flow of your individual expression shine, without comparing yourself with others. Only you get to choose what power is for you and when you choose to give it away to another person, situation or thing.

BE Your Power.

DO Powerful Acts.

HAVE a Life of Your Choice.

Remember: Be the powerful individual you are meant to be and respect others.

Invitation 61: Most of us have strong opinions on people in powerful positions. Name 3 public figures who you find to be positive examples of power?

1.

2.

3.

Invitation 62: List the top qualities these positive public figures of power represent for you.

1.

2.

3.

4.

5.

Invitation 63: Honestly ask yourself, which of these positive qualities of power do you frequently emulate? Check each of the above qualities that apply and add more qualities that you feel represent your powerful self.

Invitation 64: Looking at the qualities you checked as true for you, how often do you exert these qualities in the areas of your life that matter to you?

5	All the time
4	Frequently
3	It depends
2	Infrequently
1	Not at all

Invitation 65: Record your feelings about what you learned about yourself in your journal. List ideas for actions you may take to regain your power.

Define Power For You Tips

1. Observe how you see power in other people.

2. Be aware of your own power.

3. Accept your power.

Expand Your Learning

All of us live within three concentric circles. The innermost circle is what we know and how we choose to see the world. The middle circle is what we can learn. The outer circle is our resistance barrier. In any 'event' in life, you get to choose how to respond (or react). Do you stay within the circle that you are most familiar with? Do you stretch out your known zone by learning more about yourself? As you learn more, your resistance to new concepts and people reduces.

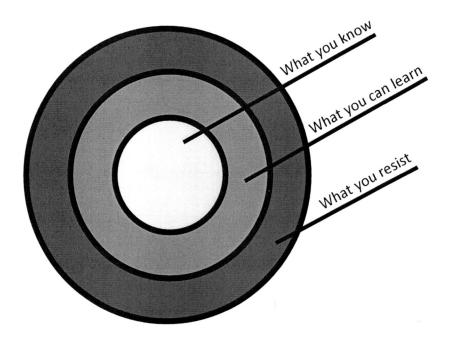

A seed breaks out of its shell to sprout, then bursts through the ground to be-come a sapling, and finally grows into a tree. It's the natural process, when not disturbed by unnatural circumstances (e.g. somebody stomping on the sprout or cutting down the tree). At no point does that seed go into resistance to the growth process. It is constantly adapting to its environment and attempting to grow. If the roots hit an obstacle, they find a way around the obstacle. If the tree does not get enough sun or nutrients, it seeks ways to grow so it can reach for those resources.

You may read this metaphor and go *"but that's not how human beings work."* I invite you to stop and think. We differ from a seed because we have been given the ability to think, to discern. Do you 100% know there is no commonality between a seed to a tree and a baby to a grown adult? We can choose to use nature as the example of how to address challenges and change to remember the natural course of our evolution is very similar.

Invitation 66: What are those events (situations) that you resist and lose your balance, your calm—either visibly to others or only internally? This can be in any situation—at work, in personal affairs, or out in public and with your friends/community.

Invitation 67: What is the frequency of these moments of resistance?

5   Daily

4   Several times a week

3   About once a week

2   2-3 times a month

1   Once a month or less often

Invitation 68: Are you concerned about the frequency of these situations?

Yes   No

Invitation 69: If yes, what have you learned about yourself that might provide new choices to consider the next time you resist a situation?

Invitation 70: Identify a pattern in events/people you resist more regularly. Choose one area to practice expanding your learning of yourself and reducing your resistance. Share your intention with someone you trust and set SMART commitments to learn from this resistance.

Panic Or Learn Tips

1. Be aware of what makes you resistant and how often.

2. Examine your beliefs underlying the resistance.

3. Expand your learning to reduce your resistance.

Your Edge

Understanding areas that cause us stress, fear and discomfort that we resist are likely the clues to growth opportunities towards creating the life of our choice. For most of us, it's much easier to point outward than take the time to look deep inside. It's uncomfortable and we avoid it. We are not trained in how to do it. However, facing those things we do not desire to confront can be the gateway to our greatest happiness. That's your edge, and some might call it a bleeding edge. Know your fears; know those things you suppress, deny and hide. Face them head on. Then charge through them anyway. It might hurt at the time but you will look back and smile with greater confidence and inner power than you imagined before. While going through such healing, never lose sight that you are perfect just as you are. You may be asking, "How do I approach learning what my true edge is and how do I learn from it?" Here are a few approaches:

- Physical events get you "into your body." Be it a ropes course event like my climbing a 50-foot pole, or doing a sports event. It provides an opportunity for your subconscious to connect to your body and bring it up to your conscious mind.

- Take the time to listen to your body. Yes, your body talks to you. The question is, do you listen? Could you ask that part of your body that is aching "what's up?" Would you stay still with an open mind and heart to listen to what emerges from within you? When done with intention, this is a powerful method of introspection.

- Observe how you respond (or react) to conflict. What do you learn from each opportunity where you feel confronted or uncomfortable? Do you run away and avoid it? Do you fight back with words or your actions? Do you brood about it internally and yet do nothing about it? Do you vent with a friend or loved one about it and still do nothing about it?

Leaning in to those moments of conflict and pushing the boundaries into trying new ways to resolve conflict is your edge. You don't need to climb a 50-foot pole or run a marathon to truly feel your edge. Each of us has numerous opportunities in our daily life to push against this self-created edge. The question is: do we choose to take that step?

Remember: Push against your edge. There lies the biggest learning and growth.

Invitation 71: Think about your past week/month. Can you recall one or more situations where you reached your edge? You might have faced conflict and likely hit resistance. Describe the situation for you to remember.

Invitation 72: How did you react or respond to the situation?

Invitation 73: What, if anything, could you do differently next time to preserve your power, reduce your resistance, and expand your knowledge of yourself?

Edge Tips

1. Be aware of your edge.

2. Seek to understand your patterns of resistance.

3. Choose what you might do differently next time.

Be comfortable with who you are.

All 101% of You!

CHAPTER 6

STEP 6:

YOUR INTEGRATION

IT'S ALL WITHIN YOU ALREADY

My Peak Event story continued...

There I was on top of the pole and the pole was shaking, at least so I thought in the beginning. It felt like I was standing on the bridge of a ship with a storm raging beneath and all around it. Fear and panic kicked in and I felt like I would lose my prize —my 100% of grabbing the trapeze bar. I was very present with the saying "it's not over till it's over."

From my feet to the top of my head it was completely clear I could not stay standing and that I would fall. My boots felt like they were falling off the little pizza-sized platform I was standing on. My knees felt weak as they banged against each other. My stomach was soft and churning. I was anything but focused except for a relentless determination to stay standing and not fall. My arms were flailing. I was desperately attempting to "get them" to balance.

In the midst of this panic, my dear friend Rob calmly called to me from below. He simply said: "Bobby, you know it's not the pole that's shaking." Wow! What a gift. That simple reminder was my turning point. I instantly knew the answer. I was shaking. I was out of balance. I was the one who could claim my own balance. I took ONE slow and steady breath. I focused on my core. By the time I had let out my breath, I realized the pole was not shaking anymore because I wasn't shaking IT any more.

It was in that moment of complete calm and bliss that I knew I had arrived at the true purpose of this exercise for me. I had this instant recognition that the exercise was 100% about my claiming my power, taking full personal responsibility and fully embracing who I am. There was the voice of "yes, I did it" and the instant knowing that this was much bigger than what I had known so far in life. I had a deep sense of gratitude for this recognition. I now knew I was close to claiming my gift—grabbing the trapeze bar and owning what I created to get there. I moved to the next step with confidence and a deep inner calm.

My Peak Event story continued on page 86.

React or Respond

An event can be anything and everything, from the birth of a child to a rash driver who pulls in front of your car suddenly. A response is how you CHOOSE to address the event. Most of us are joyous and grateful for the birth of our child. That's a relatively easy one. How about that rash driver who cuts in front of you? If you are like I was a decade ago, I'd honk at the person or flash my lights. I was REACTING.

Be aware of the distinction between reacting and responding. As situations happen around us, stay conscious of whether you react or respond. See the difference in the result you experience.

Something happens + I respond = My Experienced Result

The distinction between react and respond is quite glaring when we look at these definitions:

React (v):   to act in opposition, as against some force

Respond (v):   to correspond

If responding is corresponding:

Correspond (v):   to be in agreement or conformity

Going back to the opening example, I would be giving away my power to that driver if I reacted to what I perceive is happening. There are many alternative RESPONSES:

- Back off and let the other car do what it's doing, stay out of it's way

- Call 911 with the license plate if you feel the event is a hazard

- Pull off the road if you are angry about it and calm yourself down

Make up your own versions. Again your choice goes back to living in your power (responding) or in victim mentality (reacting). There are many outcomes down both paths and it's unlikely the response path would have many negative outcomes when you are awake to the choices you make.

Choose which emotions make you most energetic vs. those that drain your energy. We are always emoting, consciously or not. Be aware of your emotions and the way they "show up" in your choices.

Remember: Give yourself permission to stop and think of your response.

Invitation 74: Briefly describe an event/situation at work and one in your personal life where you recently reacted, rather than responded.

REACTION to Work Event	REACTION to Personal Event

Invitation 75: How did you feel after each of these events (e.g. mad, sad, or glad)? And how long were you thinking of the event/situation? In other words, how much time and energy did it take away from other things you could have been doing?

FEELINGS about Work Event	FEELINGS ABOUT Personal Event

Invitation 76: Now that you know the model of response vs. reaction, how would you choose to do these events differently if you had a "do over?"

RESPONSE to Work Event	RESPONSE to Personal Event

Invitation 77: Every time you react to a situation, journal about it. Conclude your journal entry with how you choose to do it differently next time.

React Or Respond Tips

1. Be aware when you react vs. respond.

2. Set a clear intention to stop and think before reacting/responding.

3. Dig deeper in situations when you react.

Let Go and Trust

When you plant a seed for a flower, what do you do next? You water it. You add fertilizer if necessary and you water it some more. You water it again and again and again until finally it is likely to sprout. If it doesn't, would you dig up the ground to see what's going on with the seed? That is very unlikely.

Why is it that many of us tend to dig up our mistakes and try to fix them or brood on them and punish ourselves? It just is. Even a seed planted in unfertile soil will likely not grow or take longer to grow. Once you know that, would you plant MORE seeds on the same spot? Again, that's very unlikely.

Keep this metaphor in mind the next time you are rehashing and over-analyzing what went wrong with a project, a relationship, or action you took. Definitely learn from it. Then LET IT GO. Once you've given it your best, your 101% best, let go and let the tree grow. Naturally, keep watering it and fertilizing it. Just trust that it will grow to be what it's meant to be, perfect just the way it is.

"Out beyond our ideas of right-doing and wrong-doing there is a field.

I'll meet you there."

~Rumi

Remember: Let go of past events and focus on being and doing the best you can right now.

Invitation 78: Think about a "negative" situation that you've been holding on to for quite some time. It might be resentment, or something you are resistant to face head on. Briefly describe the facts of the situation, as you see them (e.g. you were late for our meeting).

Invitation 79: Quickly write down all the emotions that come up when you are thinking of this situation. Don't hold back and put them all down (e.g. angry, mad, sad, fearful, hurt).

Invitation 80: What are your judgments about what happened (e.g. you do not respect me)?

Invitation 81: Look at the situation and ask yourself:

"Do I know for sure that my memory and perception of the "facts" of this situation are 100% correct and seen the same way by all involved?"

Yes   No

Invitation 82: Look at your feelings and ask:

"Am I willing to accept and let go of these feelings?"

Yes   No

Invitation 83: Look at your judgments and ask:

"Am I willing to accept that these are my judgments and they may not be true for others involved?

Yes   No

Invitation 84: Finally:

"Are you willing to let go of this situation or respond and ask for what you want, knowing you may not get it?

Yes   No

Make sure to journal what this exercise was like for you. What did you learn about your patterns from reviewing this situation? What can you choose to do differently in the future?

Letting Go & Trust Tips

1. Be continually aware of your nagging voices.

2. Name the pattern that emerges and let go of it.

3. Choose a new positive pattern instead.

Gratitude

It is critical to be aware of and constantly grateful for the many small things we take for granted. In prosperous nations like the United States, how many of us take time to appreciate the ease of hot running bath water in abundance, the variety of groceries from around the world and other such "basic" necessities? In many parts of the world, these basics are luxuries barely available to the most affluent in those nations.

Gratitude is the best remedy to any ailment. Gratitude starts with being aware of and celebrating your life just as it is right now. There is no need to look back or forward. Accept the perfection of where you are, even if it involves discomfort and disease at the time.

Even in situations that appear dire, a focus on gratitude is a sure anecdote to well-being vs. fear and stress. Here's a folklore story that illustrates how gratitude works:

> A farmer wins a prize cow that will bring him much fortune. The villagers come to congratulate him and are in envy of his good fortune. The farmer simply says he is grateful for this event. A few days later, the barn's gate is left open and the cow gets away. The villagers come to express their regret for the farmer's loss and he simply says again that he is grateful for having had the cow for at least some time.
>
> One day, the farmer's son loses a leg in a farming accident. The villagers come again and convey their sadness at the farmer's misfortune. The farmer is grateful that his son is still alive. Sometime later the army comes to recruit young men. They do not pick the farmer's son because of his amputated leg. The villagers come to convey how lucky the farmer is for his son not going to war and the farmer once again says he's grateful his son is well.

Yes, feel the emotions with the event and then move on. Feel grateful for everything you have.

Remember: Gratitude is being aware of the good in every moment.

Invitation 85: Start a practice of writing at least five things you are grateful for each day before going to sleep. Ideally do this practice for 30 consecutive days.

Invitation 86: Share your gratitude with at least one person each day for 30 days. Try to pick a new person each day.

Invitation 87: Now here is the iron-man version of this practice: find someone who you really think you have nothing to be grateful for. That person causes you stress. At a minimum, find at least one thing about them to be grateful for and journal about it. Kick it up a notch and speak your gratitude to them. You do not need to explain or justify why your perspective has shifted, just appreciate something about them, genuinely, that you would not have seen in the past.

Gratitude Tips

1. Be in a continuous state of gratitude.

2. Appreciate everything, big and small.

3. Apply gratitude when you are stressed.

Life is a gift.

If you do not value your gift,

nobody else will.

CHAPTER 7

STEP 7:

YOUR GIFT

CELEBRATE THE VICTORY.

My Peak Event becomes my trigger...

With a strong and calm grounding, I was ready to move forward with my pole exercise. I recalled, I was doing the exercise for myself—not for my wife, my parents, my employer, or my class mates supporting me below. The best part was I had a strong sense of ownership of the outcome, without feeling entrapped by my ego. I knew I deserved my good and I was so close to claiming it.

I had to take the next step, moving ahead from that place of calm and balance. My gift was still in the future—45 degrees to my left. I carefully lifted my left foot up and then, as I planted it down, I shuffled my right foot along. It was a few deliberate steps to point me in the direction of the trapeze bar—my gift.

There I was, finally facing the trapeze bar. I was looking at my goal (my 100%) but I had made it to that point, one step at a time. Now it was smiling at me. The trapeze bar was hanging calmly. The air was calm with only a slight breeze. The heat of the late afternoon sun was starting to fade as it got closer to sunset. I could see the hills to the West, in my peripheral view. I am so grateful that I took the time to breathe in where I was standing—on top of a 50-foot telephone pole looking out at the beauty of nature. It was better than any view I've had from the tallest buildings in the world. I was on top of the world.

It was time. I had a small voice that reminded me again that I only got one shot at this. My gut told me the gift was mine to have, if I chose to claim it. The choice was mine. I looked at the trapeze bar one last time with a deep sense of "here I come." I had visions of making a Superman-style leap. With a powerful and deliberate bounce off the pole, I flew horizontally toward the trapeze bar.

The excitement and joy of flying horizontally was fantastic. I know that I had the most brilliant smile on my face, a smile of freedom and contentment. My arms were stretched out ahead of me and my hands were wide open, ready to grab the trapeze. My legs felt tight together. My whole body felt like an arrow.

To this day, I can recall grabbing the trapeze bar. My hands went around the bar with great precision and confidence. I firmly grabbed the bar and was in complete bliss. I didn't let go. I pumped the bar several times to make sure I remembered the moment. I only let go once I felt the experience was deeply rooted in me. Once it was fully integrated in my entire being, I slowly let go and allowed my classmates who were billeting to ease me back down to the ground. Even before my feet were firmly on the ground, I had practically my entire class hugging and holding me up. I was the last of some 100 people to complete this exercise.

There was no doubt in my mind that while the experience of the pole was feeling so perfect at the time, I could choose to have this experience in any situation, without having to climb a 50-foot pole! I simply have to go inside and connect with that center.

I then realized the all-important concept of the extra Power of Inspiration, the 1%. The God of my knowing is in me, and I am simply an instrument of that divine presence, as we all are one. This became my trigger, my reminder, to tap in to in any situation when I doubt myself, when I fall into the "I can't" mind-set that I often did before this event. I seeded this Peak Event as my trigger to always remember the Power of Inspiration that flows through me all the time. I simply have to be aware that it exists and ignite it when I choose. I choose to keep the fire burning all the time and I am fortunate to have an amazing wife, family, and friends who lift me up when the flame is running low.

This and more I am destined to achieve—to give and to receive. I do not know what the universal plan is for me and I can only see as far as the next step. Knowing in that moment that all I need is accessible to me. I was in amazing peace and grace, with myself. The gravity of this recognition did not sink in as deeply at the time, as I did have a gift to claim, but the seed I planted in my consciousness of this trigger was certainly already blossoming. I had already sprinkled Miracle Grow on it!

Celebrate the Extra 1%

In the Introduction, I described the concept of the 1%. It is the unexpected delight that we never planned for or expected. When it happens it feels perfect. It works through us and those who support us. Your focus on what you want attracts the resources you need. You don't need to know or figure out "how" to get it done. That's the Power of Inspiration.

Now, at Step 7, let's illustrate how this can work so effortlessly. It comes with ease when you least expect it. Here's a personal story of how our third child, our son, arrived:

> *Our son arrived in May 2008. We call him the "five-hour baby." In December 2007, we applied to adopt a third child and then proceeded to be busy enjoying our two girls. We didn't hear a word about potential children to adopt and didn't even think about it. Then one day, we got a call at 2:00 p.m. Child services wanted to know if we were interested in a healthy two-day-old baby boy who had been abandoned at a local hospital. They were checking with other families as well. My wife and I said YES immediately. We went to the hospital with our girls to pick him up. We were home by 7:00 p.m!*

We've all had those joyous occasions where out of the blue we are delighted with the outcome. Be it the surprise visit of a loved one, an unexpected gift, an acknowledgement from someone or an organization we belong to, or an endeavor we never thought we could accomplish. This extra 1% is a reminder of the amazing things we can all do. Actually, in most cases, we need not DO anything; we simply WELCOME the flow to work through us. The key is to recognize that this power works through us, even though it may not come directly from us. These are moments when the impossible becomes possible.

Finally, the 1% represents the concept of "this or more, or better." Our conscious mind can only imagine what it is familiar with. In my personal example, all my family and I could imagine was to add a healthy boy to our family. What we received was the most joyous child who is perfectly matched with our family—physically and energetically.

Remember: Be aware of those moments of inspiration in your life.

Invitation 88: Think back to the most powerful moment of inspiration in your life. Ideally pick a time when you experienced that the impossible is possible. Describe it in as much detail as possible, here or in your journal. Make sure to include how you felt, and who was with you at the time.

Invitation 89: How did this moment/event impact you at the time it happened?

Invitation 90: How does it impact your life today, if at all?

Invitation 91: Create a trigger, a reminder to recall that time of inspiration. It can be a physical trigger or a section in your journal.

Celebrate The Extra 1% Tips

1. *Welcome the unexpected inspiration.*

2. *Allow it to flow through you.*

3. *Start to accept that anything is possible.*

Your Truth

The truth is, each of us is perfect—just the way we are. Is there room for improvement? Absolutely! Unless you first accept that you are the best you there is at this point in time, **The 101% You**, you are short-circuiting your own potential. There is always more potential waiting to be called forth, a greater you. Think of your self-evolution as moving from v1 to v2 to v2.1 to v3 and so forth.

The purpose of this workbook has been to invite more people to step up and do "their work," not their job. Work on improving yourself to be the best YOU there is. The sooner you recognize that life is simply a series of opportunities to learn and grow, the sooner you will shine in your 101% potential.

This potential can only shine when you are willing to start to tell yourself your truth. No more compromising and making do. No more "good enough." You deserve the best, and so does everyone else. We are simply at choice.

Most of us ask ourselves at some point *"who am I and why am I here?"* That is the journey of discovering your truth. Recognizing that we are all unique expressions of excellence, of something much bigger than ourselves, that is the truth. As Maryanne Williamson says: "It is our light, (our greatness) not our darkness (our weaknesses) that frightens us most." She goes on to say, "We ask ourselves—*who am I to be brilliant, gorgeous, talented, and famous? Actually, who are you not to be?*" That is at the heart of your truth, if you choose to accept it. Be aware of this truth and challenge yourself to LIVE it 101% of the time, from the big to the small things in life that matter to YOU.

"Our deepest fear is not that we are inadequate.

Our deepest fear is that we are powerful beyond measure.

It is our light, not our darkness that frightens us most.

We ask ourselves,

'Who am I to be brilliant, gorgeous, talented, and famous?'

Actually, who are you not to be?"

~Maryanne Williamson

Invitation 92: List all those qualities about yourself that make you smile. Yes, these can be your strengths and good qualities, but make sure to be smiling as you do this exercise. You KNOW what they are. They are those qualities that you delight in about yourself. The qualities when you are 100% in the flow of what you do so well, being YOU. Use your journal as we know the list will be long. Start each quality with: "I am ..."

Invitation 93: Now, honestly answer how often you live from these qualities that make you resonate, that make you shine in all the excellence you are? Remember, this is in ALL parts of your life. By Step 7 you will likely be viewing all parts of your life in balance.

5   All the time

4   Quite often but not all the time

3   It depends

2   Rarely

1   Never

Your Truth Tips

1. Be honest to yourself.
2. Be conscious of your deepest desires.
3. Delight in being the best You right now.

Your Ripple

Remember the joy you have experienced as a kid when you drop a pebble into a pond. It brought me such joy as a kid and can quickly put life in perspective now when I contemplate that visual as an adult. With each drop of a pebble, you can see the ripple reverberate out from the center until it reaches the edge. We all leave a ripple, consciously or not, with our thoughts, words and actions.

At Resonant Insights, we believe your thoughts are the ultimate beginning and the end of everything we create. As individuals, teams, and companies become aware of their internal environment—their thoughts—they can have a greater impact on the intentions they seek to create. As you think, so shall you BE → DO → HAVE, in all areas of your life.

What thoughts do you allow in to your mind? Do you consciously choose to accept those thoughts or reject them? Do you have an automatic filter that discerns what's good or bad for you? Ultimately, you are the only judge of what is good or bad for YOU! From thoughts of hatred, comparing and condemning people and situations, to the thoughts of joy, happiness and satisfaction, there is a ripple. Your thoughts ripple out all the time and you don't have control over that, unless you pay attention to your thought patterns and choose selectively.

Everything is energy—even our thoughts and emotions. Choosing to focus on positive thoughts will generate the positive energy that ripples out to the world. Now, combine the external environment and our internal environment, with this example:

> *The BP oil spill in The Gulf has impacted the external environment. There's been a lot of finger pointing on whose fault it was and how it is being handled. Many people feel it's impossible to remedy and get nature back to where it was for quite some time. The news is all about blaming and shaming those responsible.*

Imagine starting from a place of self-responsibility, and taking this approach:

Step 1: Intention   More people collectively believe a solution is possible.

Step 2: Choice   We all choose to focus 101% on the solution and not the problem.

Step 3: Commitment   Each individual commits to what they can bring to solve the problem.

Step 4: Work   We do our part (e.g. as simple as believing a solution is possible).

Step 5: Power   We remain focused on believing a solution is possible.

Step 6: Integration   We gain momentum and more "possible" solutions start to emerge.

Step 7: Gift   We get to a solution faster than when we focus on the problem.

As thoughts are preceded by actions, consider taking 101% personal responsibility for your thoughts, your words and your actions. Your ripple is creating your legacy.

Invitation 94: Make sure to do this exercise when you don't have time constraints. Ideally do it somewhere peaceful and quiet. Give yourself time to imagine this moment and feel it fully. You will need your journal again.

When you are ready, close your eyes after reading this exercise. Take a few slow and steady full breaths, in and out from your belly. Imagine you are being greeted by your "future self," yourself some twenty years from now. Be seated with your future self and imagine what he/she looks like. When you are ready, ask your future self this question: "What is my legacy? What will I be known for when I die?" Take time to listen and when you feel you are complete, open your eyes and write what you learned in your journal.

Invitation 95: Now write down three situations that you are not happy about. These situations can directly involve you or be far removed, issues of local or global consequence. They can be small or big. All that matters is that you are not happy about the situation.

1.

2.

3.

Invitation 96: As these are all "invitations," next we ask you to look at these three items and, if you are willing, to journal ways that you can step up in self-responsibility about these situations that are blocking your happiness, your joy. Remember the concept of Be → Do → Have as you approach this exercise. We hope you agree it feels different than leading with Doing.

Your Ripple Tips

1. Be aware of your ripple.

2. You are always leaving a ripple.

3. Your thoughts, words and actions are your ripple.

Your Peak Event

Most of us have had them, those times when we had such deep desire and anticipation for an outcome. Then it happens and we look back in awe and say "Wow! I did that?" It can show up in all areas of life and ranges from very physical to non-physical manifestations. That is Your Peak Event! For some it might be a physical challenge, as extreme as overcoming a terminal disease. For others it might be an intellectual accomplishment at work or school. In the end, you knew you had been successful and only your criteria of success mattered.

Peak events typically share these elements:

> **#1.** You felt it was impossible to accomplish when you set out

> **#2.** You had an intense desire and choice to accomplish the outcome

> **#3.** The event is a continuous reminder of what you can accomplish

You've been reading about my Peak Event. It brought forth the Seven Steps as a simple process that I now use with anything I want to accomplish. It sets a course and breaks it down into achievable milestones. Resonant Insights is starting a movement where people recognize the lessons within such Peak Events in their own experience, and use them as a catalyst to accomplish anything they desire.

We invite you to share your Peak Events with us. It is your defining moment that gives you that inner confidence and inspiration. We will be showcasing your stories with our community on our blog and in our newsletter, books and videos. Your sharing will definitely inspire and serve others.

If you haven't already, submit your Peak Events on our site TODAY and encourage people you know to do the same: *http://www.resonantinsights.com/resources/your-peak-event/*

Remember: Use Your Peak Events as a catalyst for having your 101% best life.

Invitation 97: Describe a challenge you felt was impossible to accomplish when you set out:

Invitation 98: Now break this event into the Seven Steps you have learned so far:

Step 1: Your Intention—what was your desired end outcome?

Step 2: Your Choice—what made it something you truly wanted?

Step 3: Your Commitment—what did you commit to and were you accountable?

Step 4: Your Work—what did you do to focus and be tenacious?

Step 5: Your Power—what did you do to face your fear and do it anyway?

Step 6: Your Integration—what made you recognize it's all within you already?

Step 7: Your Gift—what did you do to celebrate and own what you created?

Invitation 99: Create a physical reminder, a trigger, of Your Peak Event, if you don't have one already. It can be photos, a collage, a relevant item, or a physical gesture (e.g. connecting your thumb and index finger)—anything to remind you the "impossible" is possible, for you!

Your Peak Event Tips

1. Pick a Peak Event from your experiences.

2. Call upon it when faced with a challenge.

3. Use your trigger to connect with your Peak Event.

"In helping others, we shall help ourselves.

For whatever good we give out completes

the circle and comes back to us."

Flora Edwards

CHAPTER 8

YOUR CIRCLE

SUPPORT OTHERS. SUPPORT YOURSELF.

Support from my team of some 100 participants in the week-long workshop was critical to my success. I knew throughout my climbing the pole (the experience of the Seven Steps) that I was fully supported by them below. I had complete trust in them. There were at least a dozen of them (six on each side) pulling the ropes that I was connected to. I knew their eyes and full attention were on me throughout the exercise, for safety and encouragement.

Having done the same for several of my team members, in the hot California sun all afternoon, I knew how seriously we all took this responsibility. This high level of personal responsibility in service to the whole group was a given now four days into this intensive leadership training workshop. This learning happened in progression over a series of experiential exercises using our minds, hearts and gut. It didn't happen instantly. In fact, the day we arrived on the remote ranch, about three hours from the San Francisco Airport (SFO), most of us were strangers to each other. Traveling in two chartered buses from the airport was the first part of building trust and getting to know each other.

Thanks to a series of experiential exercises we did individually and collectively, we had a common understanding of many concepts. The one that was most consistent was support. I trusted my team to support me, both my physical safety and knowing that they were cheering me on. We knew that we had each other's back. I had some 100 men and women who I felt confident had my back, as I had theirs. I now try and recreate that energy of support in all areas of my life.

Create a Safe Circle

You can use the Seven Steps to create a support system, a circle of people who you support and who support you. From the beginning of humanity, we have sought and created circles of people with a common interest: cave man who banded together for safety and sustenance; religious orders for similar reasons; corporate teams with a common culture; school/college alumni, etc. The question is, is everyone truly there on their own choice and do they feel safe?

Applying the Seven Steps is one way to create a safe circle. Think of a group you are active with (work or personal) and journey through the steps below:

Step 1: Your Intention—Is there a common intention that unites everyone, something every individual will agree is the reason they are part of the circle?

Step 2: Your Choice—Are you part of this circle 100% at your own choice? Doing it out of obligation to someone else?

Step 3: Your Commitment—Are you clear about your agreements with the circle and have you committed to those agreements with them?

Step 4: Your Work—Do you know what is yours to do within this circle? How do you apply your personal mission written in the circle?

Step 5: Your Power—Do you speak your truth when you feel strongly about how things are going? Do you have the courage to stand for what you believe in?

Step 6: Your Integration—Are you in balance with how other parts of your life interact (or not) with this circle? Are they in harmony or conflict?

Step 7: Your Gift—Do you honor the strengths you bring to the circle that only you can bring? Are you willing to see this in all people in the circle?

Regardless of how advanced we may think we are as a species, our primal NEED to connect with people who we resonate with is the foundation of living our best life. People need people, just as much as we need water, food, cover and other sustaining elements nature designed into our programming.

Invitation 100: How many different communities, circles of people, do you actively participate in beyond your immediate family? And what type of communities are these?

Total number of communities I belong to are: _____

Number that are primarily sports oriented: _____

Number that are primarily about a specific cause/purpose: _____

Number that are religious or spiritually oriented: _____

Invitation 101: How often do you meet with these groups?

5   Several times a month

4   Once a month

3   Once every few months

2   Less often than every few months

1   Never

Invitation 102: How satisfied are you with the quality of these connections?

5   Extremely satisfied

4   Fairly satisfied

3   Indifferent

2   Fairly dissatisfied

1   Extremely dissatisfied

Invitation 103: Do you desire or already have the type of circle described above?

5   Desire it and already have it

4   Desire it but don't currently have it

3   Indifferent

2   Do not desire it but already have it

1   Do not desire it

Invitation 104: After evaluating your responses to the last four questions, consider creating a plan (write in your journal) to take your connections to the level you choose to. If you are already satisfied with your connections, celebrate them and find ways to go deeper. If you are not satisfied with where you are in this area of your life, dream the ideal state. Remember to start with "If **time** was not an issue, I would get more involved in _____ (types of circles)."

Create A Safe Circle Tips

1. Be aware of your support circle.

2. Call upon your circle regularly.

3. Co-create the circle of your choice.

Offer Support

Once you are part of a safe circle, a group you believe in and trust, remember that you succeed more when you support others. You might say: "but I barely have time for my own needs, how can I make time for others?" It's as simple or difficult as you choose to make it. Lean into the discomfort and do it anyway. Experience the thrill of having supported someone and saying *"Wow that was so fulfilling and easy."* Most of what I offer comes so naturally, it's very little tax on my attention, time, and energy. In fact, it's simpler than not doing it.

In order for true support to work and circulate you must first prepare yourself to put aside the *"what's in it for me?"* voice. As you practice giving support, you will experience receiving and giving even more. It is critical to offer your support unconditionally and to put your agenda aside.

There are several movements that have been founded on the concept of supporting others. The Gift (www.givethegifttoday.com) is one such example that Resonant Insights supports. Here's what The Gift is about:

Experience the Law of Contribution in your life with everyone, everywhere all the time and your life will become easy, effortless and enjoyable.

> *What makes this so compelling is just how simple it is to do. The Gift hosts networking events with a difference. Every person attending is invited to find someone in the audience they do not know. They each get ten minutes to speak and follow these four easy steps:*
>
> *1. Connect deeply with another... get interested in the person*
>
> *2. Find out what they're up to... what's one of their important goals or dreams?*
>
> *3. Contribute on the spot... offer ideas, advice, connections, support – from the heart*
>
> *4. Then watch miracles occur in your life.*

I attended one of these events and experienced this for myself. I got my first coaching client by simply asking the person I was working with. A woman who had been struggling to get her non-profit off the ground for two years happened to connect with a VC/angel funder. He, on the spot, committed to supporting her tangibly.

Remember: Support is not always a one-to-one exchange and has an element of "pay it forward."

Invitation 105: Do you agree with the concept of "support others, support yourself?" Remember, there is no right or wrong answer. Simply what is right for YOU.

> 5   Completely agree with the concept and practice it
>
> 4   Agree with the concept but don't practice it much
>
> 3   Indifferent
>
> 2   Somewhat disagree with the concept and don't practice it
>
> 1   Completely disagree with the concept and don't practice it

Invitation 106: Write your belief of what happens when you provide others unconditional support.

Invitation 107: Regardless of whether you have a positive or negative opinion of this concept, write down what keeps you from practicing unconditional support.

Invitation 108: Look around at your circle of friends, family, colleagues and acquaintances. Make a list of one thing you could do (it doesn't have to be a big commitment) for each of them and start to check-off your list with a consistent commitment (e.g. one person per day). Remember, support can be as simple as providing a relevant introduction that resonates.

Offer Support Tips

1. Connect deeply with people.

2. Put aside the voice of "what's in it for me?"

3. Give support unconditionally and often.

Receive Support

The other side of the support coin is receiving. Many of us find this much more challenging than giving support. There are many reasons for this and they vary from person to person, but it's safe to say many of us have taken on the belief that it's selfish to receive good. Learning to receive support graciously, and powerfully, is an art.

Think about the last time someone told you, "Have a great day." How did you feel? What did you do? For many of us, these gestures have become mechanical. We don't take them in and allow them to soak into our consciousness. That relatively simple act of giving a kind word is among the most powerful gestures when done sincerely. Receiving that wish from another is just such a gift. To stop and think that the other person knows you are going to have a great day.

In the reverse, think of a time when you had an argument/disagreement with someone. It likely ended with some harsh words and stressful energy. You likely carried that into your day and mulled it over in your head over and over. You sat strong in righteous indignation and had a chant of "I can't believe that person..."

Now imagine if you can put the same energy into receiving a genuine "have a great day" into your day. Every time you have a challenge, remember that this individual was wishing you have a great day. See how that feels in contrast to that negative energy.

Giving to others and receiving support is circular, not necessarily a back and forth exchange with the same person. The more of us that live this principle, the more common it will become. Revel in the surprises that will show up out of the blue when you trust in this circulation. This is fundamental to 101% and the Power of Inspiration. The Seven Steps are foundational to opening a space where this is possible. For those that have mastered these skills, dive into giving and receiving support with open arms. It will come naturally to you.

Remember: Be gracious in receiving support.

Invitation 109: Have you ever been on the receiving side of unconditional support?

YES   NO

Invitation 110: How do you feel about your answer above? Regardless of a Yes or No, how do you feel about yourself, based on this experience?

Invitation 111: What did you learn about yourself and others from this experience of receiving unconditional support? Please share your stories with us at: info@reso-nantinsights.com.

Invitation 112: Finally, on this subject of support, how many people do you feel "have your back?" And how many people know you have their back? These are rela-tionships you know you can call on at any time of day or night; and will support you unconditionally, and vice-versa.

# of people who have my back   _____

# of people whose back I have   _____

Invitation 115: Do you feel the following people have your back? Check only those that apply (e.g. skip "siblings" if you don't have any).

Significant other	Yes	No
Best friends	Yes	No
Parents	Yes	No
Siblings	Yes	No
Children	Yes	No
Manager	Yes	No
Work colleagues	Yes	No

Invitation 114: How do you feel about your response to the previous invitation?

Recieve Support Tips

1. Accept and celebrate receiving support.

2. Be clear about who has your back.

3. Create a trusted circle of support.

Grab Your Oxygen Mask

Let's bring these concepts into balance. It's fabulous to support others and you still need to care for yourself. Remember the announcement when you fly: "**If the oxygen mask falls, put your own mask on first before assisting others.**" I am useless to my kids if I die in the process of helping them with their "oxygen mask." It is my responsibility to take care of myself so I may live my life mission and support my family.

Ask yourself, do you take time for yourself? Do you set boundaries on your time and with people to make sure you are well rested, well exercised, and well fed? There are only 24 hours in a day. How do you choose to use them?

We are no good to those we serve unless we are well ourselves. There's nothing selfish about this concept. It's simply a fact. Today, self-care is just as important as survival was to our ancestors. Most of us need not fend off predators, find shelter, or hunt for our food in this modern age. But we need to view self-care as critical as survival is. Unless we nourish our mind, body and soul to replenish our batteries, we are depleted.

Do whatever it takes to create your time to nurture yourself.

Remember: You are no good to your company, your loved ones, if you are "burnt out."

Invitation 115: Pick something that's just for your self-care. Keep it simple so you can do it DAILY. Write this in your calendar or journal and check off the box each day that you do it. They say in order to change any habit we must practice the new behavior for at least 30 consecutive days. If you have made it this far on the journey of the Seven Steps and beyond, then we believe you are up for the challenge to do this for 30 consecutive days.

Invitation 116: Next, make sure to invite someone you trust to support you in accountability on this. Use the SMART commitment-setting practice to be clear about what you will do.

Invitation 117: For those who do this already or want to be challenged, pick something that's outside of your comfort zone. Ideally pick something that typically makes you feel selfish and therefore you don't do it or don't do it often. For instance, I have a wonderful wife and three kids to go home to each evening. I feel guilty to add another 1-2 hours to my day and exercise at the gym. I need support accountability to make this happen, otherwise I slack off. The more I put this in to my routine, the less guilty I feel about it. It just gets done!

Grab Your Oxygen Mask Tips

1. Be aware of your stress

2. Create frequent ways to care for yourself.

3. Make your self-care plans known to those you trust.

"Go confidently in the direction of your dreams!

Live the life you've imagined."

Henry David Thoreau

CHAPTER 9

NOT DONE TILL IT'S DONE.

Throughout the week-long leadership workshop where I did the pole exercise, many people would jump up in excitement or cry with conviction: "when I leave here I am going to change … in my life," "I am going to build … business or relationship," etc. The response from the leaders of the workshop was always very short. Actually, it was three words: "We'll see."

The words "we'll see" are simple enough and for me they were pivotal in fueling my desire to achieve what I was seeking even more. The first time one of the leaders of the workshop said these words, I took it as a personal affront. I felt they didn't believe in me and were really saying "yeah right!" Those were simply stories I made up in my own head. I later looked back at that statement as exactly what I needed at the time and, even today, it is a fuel that propels me forward. Naturally, it must come from someone you respect and trust in order to carry weight.

Remember in Step 3: Your Commitment, when I stated to one of the leaders of the workshop exactly what I wanted from the event of climbing the pole? He didn't verbalize "we'll see" at that point, and yet it was still ringing in my ears. It was a self-imposed challenge. Such challenges are more for us to ponder on and get clear about what we truly want. I was clear about what I wanted in the pole event. I put aside this prompting adage for the duration of the pole exercise.

I recognized much later that I want to use this concept of "we'll see" to energize myself. When I am clear about what I want (my intention) and I'm procrastinating, this term is a great reminder to act, to challenge myself. Having support accountability makes it even more powerful.

Prove it to yourself

Talk is cheap. Most of us agree with that common adage. Every culture has a version of it. Your actions speak volumes for what you think, what you make more important than other things, and what you truly desire. After all, by now, if you have resonated with the Seven Steps, you recognize the power of your intention in driving the rest of the journey.

How often do you feel a boss, good friend, or spouse is saying "we'll see" without actually verbalizing it? You know exactly that look on their face and their body gesture—those questions that challenge you or add doubt to whether what you intend is possible. They are usually implying they believe it's impossible, it can't be done or you haven't followed through in the past.

The first thing to recognize is that only you get to choose what you believe is possible or not. Taking on someone else's belief/disbelief does you no good. Surround yourself with people who truly believe in you. Shut out those doubting thoughts and people. They don't serve you or themselves by not believing.

You are the boss of you. Contrary to what most of us believe, in the end only you get to choose if you place value on what people think of you. How many of us can honestly say "what people think of me is none of my business" and let go of that thought? Think about how much time you spend on wondering what other people think of you. It can consume a lot of your energy, depleting it in areas where you need it to accomplish what you really want. Stay focused on what you desire and relentlessly prove it to yourself. Yes, being acknowledged by others feels good, but it's simply a bonus.

Take a look at any of the legends in leadership and success and you'll see they didn't care about proving what they stood for or their product to others. They simply believed in what, at the time, was the impossible:

- **Muhammad Yunus** a pioneering success with microcredit and eradicating illiteracy.
- **Bill Gates** "a PC on every desk."
- **Southwest Airlines** on sustaining a profitable airline.
- **Christopher Columbus** proving the world is not flat (before Thomas Freedman made it so).
- **People would fly like birds** do across continents.
- **Thomas Edison** that electricity is possible for the masses.

All it takes is the first person/company to prove it to themselves and the rest will follow because they start to believe. It all starts with ONE person believing.

Remember: Prove to yourself that what you believe is impossible is actually possible, for you.

Believe. Believe. Believe.

It's been said throughout the book, and we must add a final reminder, that it's important to believe. It is THE key ingredient in turning the impossible into the possible. We invite you to develop a plan to create the life of your choice. Never stop believing how amazing you are and what you are capable of being, doing and having. The biggest gift we can give people is to believe in them.

You can't really believe in others if you don't believe in you!

All those examples shared in the lesson on "Prove it to Yourself" would have never been possible if those legends stopped believing.

- **Muhammad Yunus** didn't give up; despite disbelievers that microcredit would work.

- **Bill Gates** didn't give up in believing the impossible of a PC on every desk

- **Southwest Airlines** didn't give up when others thought it was impossible to run a lean airline.

- **Christopher Columbus** didn't give up searching for funding for his quests.

- **The Wright Brothers** didn't give up when people thought they were crazy.

- **Thomas Edison** didn't give up, despite over 1,000 attempts.

In today's "politically correct" culture, most of us would say "I believe in you" to a young child. What stops us from saying that to an employee, a co-worker, a spouse, a friend and, most importantly, to ourselves?

Take a hard "look" at the times in your life when you have convinced yourself "I can't." Examine them to see what it is that you really desire, but have stopped believing is possible. Ask yourself what it would take to make it happen. Break it down into small steps, even fake it in the beginning until you believe it. You will look back and wonder why you were stuck, when you could easily turn the situation into an "I can." It's always your choice. You don't have to be a Thomas Edison, Bill Gates or Muhammad Yunus to believe. You simply have to believe, in yourself and others.

Invitation 118: In terms of belief, there are two schools of thought. Which one do you choose to operate from most of the time? Remember, only you know what's true for you.

Option 1: "I'll believe it when I see it."

Option 2: "I see it (in my mind) and I believe (create) it."

Invitation 119: Based on the option that is more true for you, write in your journal about how this belief serves you (or not) in the areas of your life that matter the most to you?

Be it — Do it — Have it

As we get close to the end of this workbook, let us revisit the concept of Be-Do-Have and tie it in with "we'll see." The basics from the introduction were:

- **The 101% You** is about each of us being our best.

- We live in a **Do → Have → Be** culture, almost globally.

- We tend to **compare, condemn and criticize** others and ourselves.

- **We are all unique** and have gifts to give.

- Be yourself 100% and expect the surprise 1%—The Power of Inspiration.

- When you are being you, the **doing and having falls in place.**

Invitation 120: Now is the time to really put this core concept to action. Flip through your work over the previous pages in this workbook. Congratulations on having taken the time for yourself to do this work. Now document for yourself a statement of where you were before this work and where you are/seek to be after, as it relates to be-do-have. This is your opportunity to test yourself on "we'll see!"

BEFORE:

AFTER:

*"I have been impressed with the **urgency** of doing.*

Knowing is not enough; we must apply.

Being willing is not enough; we must do."

Leonardo da Vinci

CHAPTER 10

IT IS IMPERATIVE TO EVOKE URGENCY.

One key purpose of this book is to evoke urgency. Why does it take an event like 9/11, a Tsunami, a Gulf oil spill, a hurricane or earthquake, the sudden death of a loved one, or cancer to wake us up to our constant vulnerability? Why do we shy away from connecting with others and sharing our deepest fears? Why don't we Facebook more about what's truly going on with us and instead "put on" an external face of American Idol-style showmanship" The sooner you tackle those thorns in your side that keep you from having the 100% life you desire, the more inspiration (the 1%) happens and the results you desire flow with ease.

There are many changes occurring globally that are beyond what we thought was possible: the financial market crisis, the continuing Great Recession (as some Economists have nick-named it), the environmental imperatives, not to mention the continuing wars and struggles of people in many nations. At Resonant Insights, we believe all of these challenges can be tackled when people are willing to step up and do their part, rather than pointing outward.

Each of us needs to choose: "am I a finger pointer" OR "am I about looking at what's mine to do." We can only control what is ours—our thoughts and actions. We have no control over others' thoughts and actions. As simple as that is, most of us forget to practice this principle in all areas of our lives.

Check and see if you have had these thoughts (or verbalized them):

- If only my boss/my spouse/my family would understand me...

- The government should do...

- Wall Street is to blame for our financial crisis...

The facts on any of these and a myriad of other situations really don't matter. It also doesn't matter who or what is right or wrong. All that matters is how you respond to any event that comes up for you. I love the adage "if you see a job, it's yours!" Don't complain about spilled milk, wipe it up. Don't criticize a company/boss/government about an issue, see what part you have to play in solving it and get active. If you choose not to get active, then let go of the attachment to criticizing and complaining about it. Don't underestimate your own power. If your mind goes to "but what can I do with these big/global issues?" and you think about the issue a lot, flip that question to "what is mine to do with this issue?" It could be as simple as believing a solution is possible, e.g. the Gulf oil spill can be cleaned up. And your 1% inspiration may spark an idea that you never dreamed possible. Put inspiration and yourself to the test!

Invitation 121: As a parting gift to yourself, block some time to plan YOUR next year, starting today. Start with vividly describing what your life will look like a year from TODAY. Put that date here: _____. Now journal all the details of what that will look and feel like. Don't hold back. Remember to stop/cancel those thoughts of "I can't" or "that's not possible." Dream BIG!

Invitation 122: Next, go through your one-year dream list and NOW list those barriers to making those things possible. Here are some common examples: not enough time, not enough money, or no one to support my vision. Create a master list of these first and then number each barrier. Then go back to your dream list and put the numbers that apply as barriers for each item. Look back at what you've created and notice any patterns. For instance, does "not enough time" show up consistently with all your dreams? Remember to seek feedback from your support circle.

Invitation 123: Prioritize your dream list to pick the top items you definitely want to accomplish first. Create SMART commitments for the things that will get you closer to that desired outcome. Remember to invite someone you trust to support you in accountability.

The Life of Your Choice

At Resonant Insights, we are under no illusion that not everyone desires to be a Bill Gates, a Mahatma Gandhi, a Muhammad Yunus, an Oprah or a Bono. It isn't about the public bigness of these legends that we are about. It's about their impact!

There are endless examples of people and companies that most of us have never heard of that are having a profound impact on their world. Here are just a few examples that you are likely living or know someone who is:

- The mother 100% dedicated to the care of her little children.

- The son who's 100% dedicated to the care of a father with Alzheimer's.

- The friend who's 100% dedicated to supporting a family whose house burned to ashes.

- The man who loves music and is 100% dedicated to teaching children the piano.

- The breast cancer survivor who's 100% dedicated to supporting a cure.

- A corporate employee 100% dedicated to inspiring his co-workers.

- A nine year-old boy 100% dedicated to providing clean water in Africa.

Many of us postpone our dreams, our deepest desires and wishes for ourselves and the world. We look to others to do them, live vicariously through them, and sit in the bleachers observing. Ask yourself:

"If not now, when? If not me, who?"

Remember: Seeking 100% is about being your best, not about perfection.

Invitation 124: These final few invitations are truly about self-mastery. Do not attempt them if you are not ready and we challenge you to view them with urgency.

What impact would you like to have on the world, your world? What do you want your legacy to be? Maybe you've created much of this already—congratulations! And what else is there to create before you take your last breath?

Invitation 125: What's in the way of you having that impact right NOW? What's the delay?

Invitation 126: Now, if you are willing, similar to Invitations 27-28, create a SMART plan in these areas where you want to have more impact.

Remember: You can do well, for yourself and others, as a "for profit" person/organization. Break the walls.

"Here is the test to find whether your mission on earth is finished: If you're alive, it isn't."

Richard Bach

Call to Action

Ways to Continuously Live 101%™ the Life of Your Choice individually, with your team and your organization.

Employee Engagement Advisors

We customize programs with leaders and their teams to address ways to increase employee engagement. We provide fresh perspectives on how to live a culture focused on strengths. We connect your individual and team commitments with a focus on: INTENTIONS, DRIVE and EXCELLENCE.

Be 101% Metrics™

Be 101% Metrics™ is our online well-being tool packed with resources for your team in six key areas of life. It provides:

- Confidential assessment

- Resources to shift behavior

- Set commitments

- Challenge each other

- Track progress

Coaching

We work with individuals and teams to turn the impossible to the possible from within. We start by inspiring a connection with purpose.

We evoke the best in people by asking questions that integrate all parts of who you are.

We apply our 7 Steps process to anchor your peak events, those times when you achieved the impossible.

Experiential Events

Our workshops take a radically different approach to getting things done. Our foundational events focus on an individual's state of being. Once we set that base understanding of what you truly want, we definitely get things done and set you up to have great results. However, the journey can be full of fun, passion and purpose—if you choose.

First, Get Clear

Discover what drives your individual and team's decision making and the impact it has on your results. A 3-4 hour experiential team event.

Next: Go Deep

Apply what you learn to an existing project and achieve *Big High Audacious Intentions* (BHAI).

A 3 month commitment, meeting every 2-weeks during your regular team meetings.

Finally: Live it 101%

Learn how to sustain a Be-Do-Have perspective in the areas of your life that matter the most to you.

A one-day commitment, as a team or individually.

For more information, visit www.resonantinsights.com or email us at info@resonantinsights.com

Join the Tribe

Join our movement of positive change.

Weekly Invitations

Sign up for our free newsletter to receive simple tips each week. We invite subscribers to practice the lessons each week and share your experience with the Resonant Insights Tribe. Sign up today at our site **www.resonantinsights.com**

Share Your Peak Events

Fill our short form and share Your Peak Events with the world. Visit our site often to read Peak Events and be inspired by people like You, turning the impossible to the possible.

Topical Webinars

Check often for a series of webinars to go deeper on how to cultivate sustainable employee engagement within your team and your organization.

Join the Conversation

Last but not least... we would love for you to comment on all our social networks and to send us relevant content to share with our global community. We are on:

Facebook | LinkedIn | Twitter | Slideshare | You Tube

Inspire others, inspire yourself.

Support others, support yourself.

Resonant
Insights
PUBLISHING

Visit www.resonantinsights.com to Be Your 101%!

Summary of Tips

Step 1: Your Intention

Desire

1. Be awake to your deepest desires.

2. Accept your desires without judgment.

3. Be honest, don't settle.

Belief

1. Listen to your inner voices.

2. Be aware of what you choose to believe.

3. Be open to believing anything is possible.

Result

1. Be focused on your desired outcome.

2. Let go of the attachment to the outcome.

3. Give it time to grow and stay persistent.

Blockers

1. Be aware of your blockers.

2. Choose to turn blockers to positives.

3. Stay vigilant to the blocker voices.

Step 2: Your Choice

Choice Just Is

1. Remember, you are always at choice.

2. Only YOU make choices for you.

3. Be aware of how you feel about your choices.

Own Your Choice

1. Recognize when you do or don't own your choice.

2. Embrace the power of your choice.

3. Frequently examine how you feel about your choices.

Self-Responsibility

1. Be conscious to your part in any situation.

2. Discern what is and is not in your control.

3. If it's out of your control, ask for what you want.

Step 3: Your Commitment

Accountability

1. Be clear WHY you commit.

2. Be conscious WHAT you commit to.

3. Apply SMART to commitments you choose.

Your Witness

1. No one can hold you accountable; they can only support you in accountability.

2. Identify people you trust to witness and support your commitments.

3. Be conscious of your commitments: who, why, how, what and when.

Regret-Free

1. Be aware of your regrets.

2. Choose the regrets you wish to do something about.

3. Let go of the regrets you choose to leave behind.

Falling Short

1. Be true to yourself when you feel you fall short.

2. Check what beliefs are underneath this feeling of falling short.

3. Be open to welcoming that YOU CAN accomplish this, if you choose.

Step 4: Your Work

What's Yours To Do

1. Be clear about what your "work" is.

2. Examine WHY you do what you do.

3. Recognize and celebrate your uniqueness.

You Spot it You Got it

1. Recognize the mirror others are for you.

2. It is your pattern you see in others.

3. Recognize your pet peeves are about you.

Grow or Decay

1. Evaluate your choices as generative or decaying.

2. Remind yourself of your Peak Event when faced with a challenge.

3. Keep your focus on your intention to pull you forward.

Focus One Step at a Time

1. Decide what's important to focus on.

2. Determine what's stopping you.

3. Create a commitment plan to get it done.

Step 5: Your Power

Courageous

1. Be aware of the feelings you are denying yourself.

2. Choose to walk through your fears courageously.

3. Start with small things to test the waters.

Trusting Your Gut

1. Listen for your inner voices.

2. Be aware if you accept or deny your gut.

3. Trust your gut instincts.

Define Power for You

1. Observe how you see power in other people.

2. Be aware of your own power.

3. Accept your power.

Panic or Learn

1. Be aware of what makes you panic and how often.

2. Examine your beliefs underlying the resistance.

3. Expand your learning to reduce your resistance.

Your Edge

1. Be aware of your edge.

2. Seek to understand those situations you resist.

3. Choose what you might do differently next time.

Step 6: Your Integration

React or Respond

1. Be aware when you react vs. respond.

2. Set a clear intention to stop and think before reacting/responding.

3. Dig deeper in situations when you react.

Letting Go & Trust

1. Be continually aware of your nagging voices.

2. Name the pattern that emerges and let go of it.

3. Choose a new positive pattern instead.

Gratitude

> 1. Be in a continuous state of gratitude.
>
> 2. Appreciate everything, big and small.
>
> 3. Apply gratitude when you are stressed.

Step 7: Your Gift

Celebrate the Extra 1%

> 1. Welcome the unexpected inspiration.
>
> 2. Allow it to flow through you.
>
> 3. Start to accept that anything is possible.

Your Truth

> 1. Be honest to yourself.
>
> 2. Be conscious of your deepest desires.
>
> 3. Delight in being the best You right now.

Your Ripple

> 1. Be aware of your ripple.
>
> 2. You are always leaving a ripple.
>
> 3. Your thoughts, words and actions are your ripple.

Your Peak Event.

> 1. Pick a Peak Event from your experiences.
>
> 2. Call upon it when faced with a challenge.
>
> 3. Use your trigger to connect with your Peak Event.

Step 8: Your Circle

Create a Safe Circle

1. Be aware of your support circle.

2. Call upon your circle regularly.

3. Co-create the circle of your choice.

Offer Support

1. Connect deeply with people.

2. Put aside the voice of *"what's in it for me?"*

3. Give support unconditionally and often.

Receive Support

1. Accept and celebrate receiving support.

2. Be clear about who has your back.

3. Create a trusted circle of support.

Grab Your Oxygen Mask

1. Be aware of your stress.

2. Create frequent ways to care for yourself.

3. Make your self-care plans known to those you trust.

About the Author

With a life mission to "empower a world of compassion, courage and abundance by evoking the best in people," Bobby Bakshi constantly seeks ways of being 101% true to his mission. He lives this mission with several organizations and communities he serves, starting with his family of three little children and wife Judy.

Bobby Bakshi founded Resonant Insights LLC, a leadership and employee engagement advisory firm. His first book, **THE 101% YOU**, is tied with the launch of Bobby's firm.

Bobby applies his experience of several leadership and personal growth programs over the past decade. Everything he designs to teach in workshops, consulting and products, he has lived in his own life. He takes the knowledge of many sciences and brings it to the global workforce with urgency and relevance for immediate application.

A marketing research professional of over two decades, Bobby has worked at Fortune 100 companies and led marketing strategy for many well-known technology brands. Bobby is passionate about the intersection of marketing and human capital, that leads to a deeper understanding of people's true desires.

Contact Bobby directly at: bobby@resonantinsights.com.